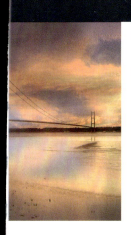

A JOURNEY THROUGH THE LIFE OF

# William Wilberforce

*the abolitionist who changed the face of a nation*

by **KEVIN BELMONTE**

*Leading Wilberforce scholar and consultant
for the movie* Amazing Grace

New Leaf Press
First Printing: January 2007

ISBN-13: 978-0-89221-671-0
ISBN-10:    0-89221-671-9
Library of Congress Number: 2006937540

Previously published in Great Britain as *Travel with William Wilberforce,
The Friend of Humanity*; Kevin Belmonte, author; Brian H. Edwards,
series editor; by Day One Publications, Leominster, Great Britain, 2006,
www.dayone.co.uk.

Cover and interior design by Rebekah Krall

Printed in the United States of America

For information regarding author interviews, please contact the publicity
department at (870) 438-5288.

Please visit our website for other great titles: www.newleafpress.net

**New Leaf Press**
*A Division of New Leaf Publishing Group*

# Acknowledgments

Many have helped in the preparation of this book, but I must single out the following friends, and institutions — without whom this book would not have been possible. Brian Edwards and Marylynn Rouse have provided indispensable editorial and photographic assistance. Steve Devane has wedded the pictures into a superb graphic design and layout. The Wilberforce House Museum in Hull (one of Britain's national treasures) has extended many courtesies to me, and allowed me the use of some wonderful images. I am deeply indebted to Ms. Vanessa Salter, the Keeper of Social History for the Hull Museums, and her colleagues there. In America, Jeremy Burnham and his colleagues at Eagle Photo have gone above and beyond the call of duty. Lastly, I feel a sincere and lasting sense of gratitude to Day One Publications for according me the privilege of writing this book.

# Contents

# William Wilberforce:
## One of the Great Souls of History

William Wilberforce (1759–1833) has been called "the greatest reformer in history." Best-remembered for leading the 20-year fight to abolish the British slave trade, this victory was itself described by the distinguished historian G.M. Trevelyan as "one of the turning events in the history of the world." Deeply important as his abolitionist labors were, it must be remembered as well that Wilberforce also supported or led some 70 different philanthropic initiatives — projects ranging from child labor laws to the education of the blind and the deaf. He funded hospitals and schools with his own money and founded organizations as diverse as the Royal Society for the Prevention of Cruelty to Animals (RSPCA) and the National Gallery (of Art). "Good causes," it has been said, "stuck to him like pins to a magnet."

But he was also one of the great souls of history — for his passionate pursuit of social justice flowed from his faith. Where Dr. Martin Luther King Jr. had spoken in his timeless "I Have a Dream" speech of "a beautiful symphony of brotherhood" — Wilberforce had, 155 years before, written of a "concert of benevolence" in an abolition letter to President Thomas Jefferson. In words that Dr. King would have understood well, Wilberforce had also written: "In the Scriptures no national crime is condemned so frequently, and few so strongly, as oppression and cruelty, and the not using our best endeavours to deliver our fellow-creatures from them."

Wilberforce's influence was deeply felt, not only in Britain, but also in America and beyond. Leaders from his own day and leaders closer to our own have been shaped by his legacy. Harriet Beecher Stowe praised him in the pages of *Uncle Tom's Cabin*. Novelist E.M. Forster compared him to Gandhi. Abraham Lincoln invoked his memory in a celebrated speech. In the houses of Parliament, Nelson Mandela recalled his tireless labors on behalf of the sons and daughters of Africa, calling Britain "the land of William Wilberforce — who dared to stand up to demand that the slaves in our country should be freed."

And yet this legacy nearly never was. It was only after Wilberforce underwent what he later described as his "great change," or embrace of Christianity, that he became a reformer. This transformation was at the heart of the true story behind the hymn "Amazing Grace." For it was John Newton, the hymnwriter and parson who had once been a slave ship captain — a man guilty of crimes against humanity — who became Wilberforce's spiritual counselor and set his young protégé on the path of service to humanity. Invoking the deliverance language of the Old Testament Book of Esther, Newton told Wilberforce that it was for "such a time as this" that he had been placed in a position as a powerful Member of Parliament to secure the abolition of the slave trade. It was in the House of Commons, Newton stated, that he could best serve God.

There is something deeply stirring about a life lived in service to something larger than self. When we view such a life, we are reminded anew of the longing so many have to live lives that count — lives that have meaning. Wilberforce devoted his life to ending the British slave trade — this though he had never been to Africa. In later years he championed the cause of emancipation throughout Britain's colonies. In 1833, as he was gravely ill, he learned that 800,000 slaves would be freed. He died three days later. His life and his legacy have much to teach us still. These pages are intended to commend something of that life to the reader and to convey the enduring truth that we ourselves can live our lives in service to God and in service to others. It is as Nobel Laureate Desmond Tutu said in June 2005: "Wilberforce showed that each and every one of us can make a difference."

For the past five years, I have been privileged to serve as the Lead Historical Consultant for the film *Amazing Grace*. Working with the screenwriter, Steven Knight, was a particular pleasure. He has a gift for distilling the dramatic essence of a story, especially an epic story like Wilberforce's. The commitment of the production team to crafting a film worthy of Wilberforce, and those with whom he worked, was also clearly evident throughout. Hearing director Michael Apted compare Wilberforce to Nelson Mandela during a visit to the set of the film was memorable for me, as was meeting Ioan Gruffudd, who plays Wilberforce. His kindness and deep interest in all the facets of Wilberforce's character, faith, and humanity was something I won't soon forget.

As for the ways in which film can affect our culture, I would say that excellently made films can be catalysts for important and instructive discussions about art, history, and the making of a better world. May this book also help foster such discussions — about the life and legacy of William Wilberforce — and the making of a better world.

Kevin Belmonte
*Author*

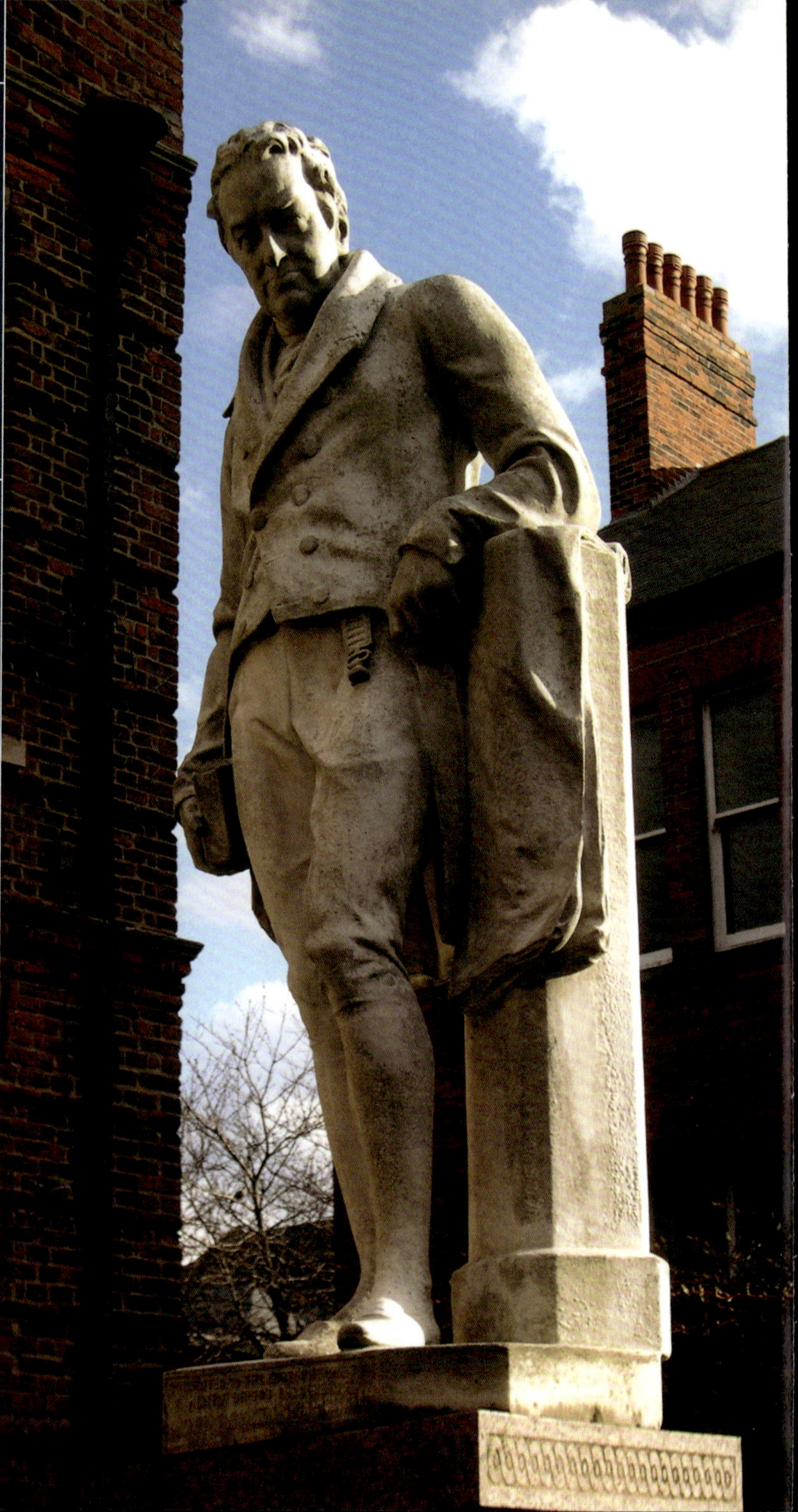

# Introduction: MEET WILLIAM WILBERFORCE

London 1817. The Italian statesman Count Pecchio was present for the start of a new session of Parliament. As he watched, one event fastened itself upon his memory: the arrival of William Wilberforce. "When Mr Wilberforce passes through the crowd," Pecchio observed, "every one contemplates this little old man, worn with age, and his head sunk upon his shoulders, as a sacred relic; as the Washington of humanity."

Wilberforce had led the 20-year fight to end the British slave trade. It was a victory known the world over. He had persevered despite death threats, chronic illness, and the long war against Napoleon's France. Yet Wilberforce was no dour, stodgy icon. Rather, friends and family were hard put to adequately describe his winsome personality. Historian Sir James Mackintosh perhaps said it best: "I never saw anyone who touched life at so many points." Mackintosh was commenting three years before Wilberforce's death. He had, along with so many others, witnessed Wilberforce's unceasing charitable interests. A conservative estimate puts the number of these at 70. Educational reform, better working conditions in factories, legislation for the poor, public health initiatives — these and many more had been the focus of his parliamentary life.

Mackintosh had also known the character of the man — as at ease with children as with statesmen — and whose natural eloquence was described by Prime Minister William Pitt as "the greatest I have ever known."

Wilberforce's last victory came two days before his death. At long last, slavery itself would be abolished throughout Britain's colonies. His legacy lives on today. Colleges and universities bear his name. For kings, presidents, and many others, his life remains a beacon — representative of a persistent and genuine commitment to principled leadership.

---

FACING PAGE: The Wilberforce memorial statue, located in the front garden of the Wilberforce House Museum, Hull. "England owes to him the reformation of manners. The world owes to him the abolition of slavery."

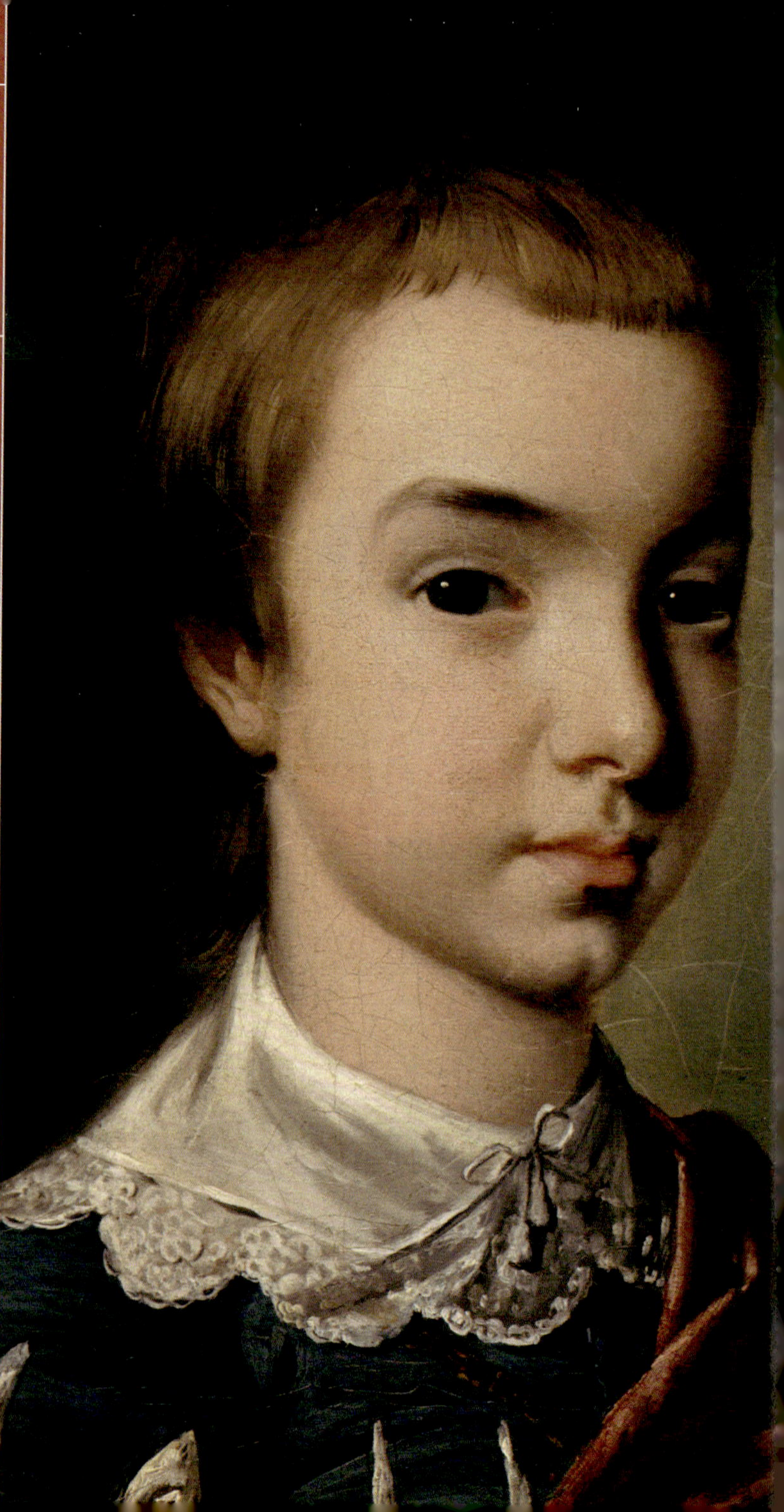

# chapter 1 ▪ BEGINNINGS

**What makes for a great social reformer? Wilberforce's youth, at times troubled, was marked by contrasts. He found a boyhood hero and knew heart-rending losses. Yet all the while, as he later said, "a gracious hand leads us in ways that we know not."**

William Wilberforce could proudly trace his ancestry back to the 12th century. Under King Henry II, Ilgerus de Wilberfoss had served in the Scottish wars, and successive generations resided in the township of Wilberfoss, eight miles east of York, from which the family had taken its surname. A branch of the family moved to Beverley around the middle of the 16th century, and some years later, at the opening of the great rebellion against Charles I that led to the English Civil War, a William Wilberfoss served as mayor of Beverley. The same office was filled twice in the city of Hull in the north of England by his great-grandson, also named William Wilberfoss, or, as he fixed its spelling, Wilberforce. Alderman Wilberforce, as he was known, had inherited a sizable family fortune derived from the Baltic trade. He was also heir to considerable landed property. The younger of his two sons, Robert, served as a partner in the family merchant house in Hull. It was here that Robert's son William, the future reformer, was born on August 24, 1759.

The year 1759 is now remembered as Britain's annus mirabilis, or year of wonders. It had been a year of victories during the conflict with France known as the Seven Years'

BELOW: The River Humber, Hull, as it is now. Wilberforce walked and played along its shores as a boy.

FACING PAGE: Wilberforce, age 11. Portrait by John Russell, 1770.

War. Battles had been won on land at Quebec and Minden and at sea off Lagos and at Quiberon Bay. Forces under the leadership of General Wolfe and Admiral Hawke had achieved victories that seemed to verge on the miraculous.

Culturally speaking, this was the year in which the British Museum opened its doors to the public for the first time, and in which the Scottish poet, Robert Burns, was born. It was also the year which witnessed the birth of William Pitt the Younger, later to become prime minister. In the years to follow, Pitt and Wilberforce would develop a deep and lasting friendship, one of great significance for Britain.

The Wilberforce family lived in a red-brick Jacobean mansion located on High Street, Hull. Although Wilberforce's grandfather, the alderman, owned land in the regions around Hull and the estate of Markington near Harrogate, the family had no great country house. The High Street mansion was the center of family life. Finely cooked meals were served in the elegant oak-paneled dining room, and guests would pass through a handsome archway that allowed passage from the front to the rear of the residence; there were attractive walled gardens in the front and rear of the house for a boy to play in.

Midway down the archway on the right was the main entry into the mansion. Upon entering, the visitor immediately saw a wide, grand, and graceful staircase that led to the home's most prominent rooms. Overhead was a beautiful Wedgwood blue ceiling, with white bas relief-sculpted edgings. Just below this ceiling was the great black eagle that served as the family crest. Exquisite taste and refined gentility were the lasting

ABOVE: William and Hannah Wilberforce portrait in the Wilberforce House Museum.

14

ABOVE: Wilberforce's birthplace, Hull, now the Wilberforce House Museum.

impressions that all this conveyed. Here lived a family that had attained prominence and wealth.

LEFT: Detail of Blue Plaque, Hull Grammar School.

It was from here that young Wilberforce, starting at the age of eight, would walk to the Hull Grammar School. It was a school of distinction, numbering among its former students the 17th century poet and politician Andrew Marvel. As an only son and future heir to his father's substantial fortune, Wilberforce's education was undertaken with care. His relationship with his father in particular was close. William attended the Hull Grammar School as a day-boy for two years. Though small, he took an active part in sports and showed signs of having a first-rate mind. Even at such a young age, his elocution so impressed his 17-year-old tutor, Isaac Milner, that he was made to stand on a table and asked to read aloud, as an example to his fellow students. Holidays were special times, too. He would then visit Alderman Wilberforce in Ferriby, a village seven miles distant, along the River Humber.

## Painful Partings

Tragically, in the summer of 1768, just before his ninth birthday, Wilberforce's father died. It was the second death of a loved one in a year, the first being that of his eldest sister Elizabeth, age 14. His mother, also named Elizabeth, was expecting another child, and following the death of her husband, Robert, she became gravely ill; fearing the worst, it was decided (very likely by the alderman) that Wilberforce would go to live with his father's elder brother, another William, who lived in London at St. James' Place.

A touching account of Wilberforce's boyhood sensitivity has survived. It dates from about the time of his father's death. A family friend who frequently stayed at the High Street mansion, and was once taken ill while there, observed that, "An unusual thoughtfulness for others marked his youngest childhood. I shall never forget how he would steal into my sickroom, taking off his shoes lest he should disturb me, and with an anxious face look through my curtains to learn if I was better."

Uncle William and his wife Hannah were childless, and so they lavished love on their grieving nephew and made him their heir. Wilberforce developed a particular fondness for their country home in Wimbledon at Lauriston House. When he came of age some years later, their Queen Anne-style villa was bequeathed

BELOW: The grand staircase of the Wilberforce House.

BELOW: The oak-paneled dining room of the Wilberforce House.

to him. It was an elegant home, situated on five and one-half acres on the south side of Wimbledon Common and within easy walking distance of Rushmere Pond. Architecturally, it was distinguished by tall windows on both of the main floors. Inside, the staircase walls and ceiling were graced with murals painted by the noted Russian artist Angelica Kauffman. It was an altogether welcoming place. Sadly, the villa no longer exists, but its handsome coach house remains. A blue plaque has been placed there in Wilberforce's memory.

BELOW: Model of the slave ship *Brookes,* used by Wilberforce as a visual aid for speeches in the House of Commons.

Standards for private education often varied widely in the late 1700s, and the school in Putney at which Wilberforce was now placed was said to have been "of the meanest character." It left a vivid impression on young William:

ABOVE: Detail of the black eagle, the emblem of the Wilberforce family crest.

Mr. Chalmers the master, himself a Scotchman, had an usher of the same nation, whose red beard — for he scarcely shaved once a month — I shall never forget. They taught writing, French, arithmetic, and Latin . . . with Greek we did not much meddle. It was frequented chiefly by the sons of merchants, and they taught therefore everything and nothing. Here I continued some time as a parlour boarder: I was sent at first amongst the lodgers, and I can remember even now the nauseous food with which we were supplied, and which I could not eat without sickness.

Wilberforce remained two years at this school. Holidays were spent at Lauriston House, with occasional visits to Nottingham and Hull. His time at the Putney school left him with no bonds of lasting affection, but the faith of his aunt and uncle did. Both had been deeply influenced by the popular evangelical preacher George Whitefield.

This was the period of English history that has become known as the Great Awakening. A spiritual revival was sweeping across the land, fueled by the preaching of men like George Whitefield and the founder of Methodism, John Wesley, and in Wales, Howell Harris. There is little doubt that this widespread revival of true Christian faith not only held back England from the revolution and anarchy that plagued France toward the end of the century, but also prepared the ground for the two great causes that Wilberforce would later take up as his life's work.

## Isaac Milner (1750–1820)

Just nine years older than Wilberforce, Isaac Milner was an imposing figure whose academic distinctions were significant. In recognition of his skills as a scientist, he was later elected to the prestigious Royal Society. He also served as vice chancellor of Cambridge University.

Isaac possessed great physical strength and intellectual gifts. In appearance and manner, he reminded many who knew him of Samuel Johnson. He had a stentorian voice, a love of truth and debate — and great intellectual curiosity. In other ways Milner also resembled Johnson — in "the warmth of his affection and the tenderness of his sympathy." His letters revealed what many came to know in person: "the constancy of his friendships."

Isaac Milner had been apprenticed to a weaver as a boy, but through hard work and great determination, he had gone on to earn much acclaim at Cambridge. Aside from the accomplishments already listed, he eventually served as president of Queen's College and as a member of the prestigious Board of Longitude.

ABOVE: The coach house of Wilberforce's home in Wimbledon, Lauriston House. The plaque below was placed there in his memory.

All the available evidence suggests that Wilberforce never met the great evangelist, Whitefield, but he grew close to someone who had been greatly influenced by Whitefield, and who would have a great influence on his life: the former slave-ship-captain-turned-parson, John Newton. It was Newton's practice to regularly visit the Wilberforce home to conduct what he called "parlor preaching." During one series of parlor sermons, Newton is known to have expounded John Bunyan's *Pilgrim's Progress* to William and Hannah Wilberforce and their guests.

Young William listened at length to stories of Newton's days at sea, and he was deeply drawn to the warm character of the former captain. Newton's kindness, along with the love and attention he received from his uncle and aunt, had its effect upon the young Wilberforce. His letters home to his recovering mother began to show a distinctly religious tone.

But his mother and grandfather would have none of that. "If Billy turns Methodist, he shan't have a sixpence of mine," his grandfather declared. His mother, meanwhile, was dispatched to Wimbledon to bring her boy home. Wilberforce remembered, "I deeply felt the parting, for I loved them as parents. Indeed, I was almost heartbroken at the separation." He wrote to his uncle, "I can never forget you as long as I live."

## How a Gentleman Ought to Be Raised

When mother and son returned to Hull, she and the alderman set about scrubbing his soul clean of Methodism, which was considered in polite society to be nothing more than excessive enthusiasm. Newton's parlor sermons were replaced with a constant round of visits to the neighboring gentry. Wilberforce recalled that the theater, balls, great suppers, and card parties were the delight of the principal families in the town. The usual dinner hour was two o'clock, and at six they met for sumptuous suppers. This kind of life was at first

### George Whitefield

Though Wilberforce himself probably never met Whitefield (1714–1770), his ministry had a profound impact on the Wilberforce family.

Wilberforce's Uncle William and Aunt Hannah had been converted under Whitefield's ministry. They counted Whitefield among their close friends, and he often visited them at their home in Wimbledon, Lauriston House. Hannah Wilberforce's half-brother, the wealthy financier John Thornton, was also converted through Whitefield's ministry in 1754. As with in the Wilberforce home, Whitefield preached frequently in Thorton's home, a handsome villa in Clapham.

It is easy to see why the Wilberforce family and John Thornton would have been drawn to Whitefield. He was, by any measure, a fascinating man. Called "the divine dramatist" by one writer, his powerful voice and heartfelt manner had a compelling effect on those who heard him. As well as the "parlor meetings" in wealthy homes, huge crowds gathered to listen to him in the open air. His uniqueness as a preacher also sprang from his ability to speak extemporaneously, rather than reading his sermons from notes. This natural form of address was in itself winsome. No less an authority than the popular 19th century preacher C.H. Spurgeon wrote memorably of the qualities that drew people to Whitefield: "Often as I have read his life, I am conscious of distinct quickening whenever I turn to it. He lived. Other men seemed to be only half-alive; but Whitefield was all life, fire, wing, force."

ABOVE: Wooded meadow, Putney Heath, a place well known to the young Wilberforce.

distressing to him. His religious impressions continued for a considerable time after his return to Hull but since, as he put it, "no pains were spared to stifle them," they slowly ebbed away. Gradually, distress gave way to acceptance, and acceptance gave way to a great interest in all that was held out before him. It could hardly have been otherwise, for he was "everywhere invited and caressed."

Wilberforce had also been placed, soon after his return to Hull, with the Rev. Kingsman Baskett, master of the endowed grammar school of Pocklington. Baskett had formerly been a Fellow of St. John's College, Cambridge, and was described as "a man of easy and polished manners

— an elegant though not profound scholar." As grandson to one of the principal inhabitants of Hull, Wilberforce was treated at Pocklington with unusual liberality. He boarded in the master's house and generally led a life of idleness and pleasure.

Nevertheless, signs of the man he would later become were not totally absent. He was said to have inherited his mother's intellectual gifts. Despite his lack of discipline, he cultivated a taste for literature, and committed passages of English poetry to memory. His favorite poem was "The Minstrel" by James Beattie, which he learned by heart during his morning walks. Poetry and walks would always provide him with much pleasure and encouragement. Wilberforce also proved to be a good writer, and though, as one classmate remembered, he seldom began writing his compositions till the 11th hour, he always excelled the other boys.

Kingsman Baskett's ties to St. John's College very likely proved the deciding factor in Elizabeth Wilberforce's decision to send her son there. Since she and the alderman cherished hopes that William would further increase the family fortune and its prestige, it would be no bad thing if he turned out more or less like Baskett. Such a man would certainly retain the family's eminence among the great families of Hull, and perhaps he might even obtain a position in Parliament. Either way, Elizabeth was leaving nothing to chance. She had decided upon St. John's, and

BELOW: Statue of an unfettered slave at the Pocklington School. Wilberforce's memory and legacy is cherished there.

BELOW: The Pocklington School. Wilberforce grew close to the headmaster, Kingsman Baskett, visiting him in later years.

ABOVE: Wilberforce within a few years of leaving university.

St. John's it would be. But if Elizabeth Wilberforce thought her son safely on course for the future that she and the alderman planned for him, events would soon prove that he was very nearly diverted from it.

By the time he went up to university in October 1776, William was a thorough religious skeptic. He had no strong sense of moral principles to guide his course, and by the death of his uncle he had been left "the master of an independent fortune." This would prove fateful. "On the very first night of my arrival," he recalled, "I was introduced to as licentious a set of men as can well be conceived. They drank hard, and their conversation was even worse than their lives. I lived amongst them for some time." Wilberforce's first days at St. John's College, Cambridge, were spent by his own admission, in "shapeless idleness." He gambled, drank, and danced the nights away.

On the other hand, during that first year at St. John's, Wilberforce confessed that he was often horror-struck at the conduct of his companions. He resolved to shake off his connection with them and decided to spend more time among the Fellows of the college, perhaps owing in part to the friendship he shared with Kingsman Baskett. The kind of life he had known at Pocklington was more familiar, and very likely a good deal more comfortable because it was a known quantity. There was something about the lives of his early, dissolute friends that was unsettling. Though drawn to it at first, he now instinctively shied away from it. This decision separated Wilberforce from friends who might have encouraged him to become a rake, but it was not an about-face. Rather, it was a decision to resume the kind of holding pattern he had done at Pocklington: a bit more polish to his manners, and occasional forays into English literature, or the Greek and Roman classics, as his fancy dictated.

The Fellows at Cambridge did nothing to discourage this tendency. Wilberforce recalled, "Their object seemed to be to make and keep me idle. If ever I appeared studious, they would say to me, 'Why in the world should a man of your fortune trouble himself with fagging [tedious study]?'" Wilberforce could later claim, "I acquitted myself well in the college examinations; but mathematics, which my mind greatly needed, I almost entirely neglected, and was told that I was too clever to require them. Whilst my companions were reading hard and attending lectures, card parties and idle amusements consumed my time. The tutors would often say within my hearing, that 'they were mere saps, but that I did all by talent.' This was poison to a mind constituted like mine."

BELOW: King's College, Cambridge.

Wilberforce was also ambitious, keenly so, and this was a further reason why he applied himself to reading literature and the Greek and Roman classics. His sense of ambition was

ABOVE: The Round Church, a hallowed and historic site which cherishes Cambridge's Christian heritage.

ABOVE: John Thornton, one of the 18th century's great philanthropists and a mentor to the young Wilberforce.

fired also in the last year or so of his time at Cambridge by newer friendships he made with young men like William Pitt, the son of Lord Chatham who was the former prime minister known as the "Great Commoner." Other friends were sons of the nobility or of members of Parliament. Gradually, Wilberforce began to see himself taking a place in the House of Commons with them. It was not unthinkable, since one of his cousins had already secured election to Parliament, and William thought it a great thing. He now made sure he applied himself enough to his studies so as to avoid being disgraced should he embark on a career in public life. If he chose this path, he had no need to work to gain a substantial income. Inherited wealth had seen to that.

So, by the time Wilberforce concluded his studies at St. John's, he had decided what he wanted. He would not be a partner in his family's merchant house. Quite another course beckoned: a career in politics.

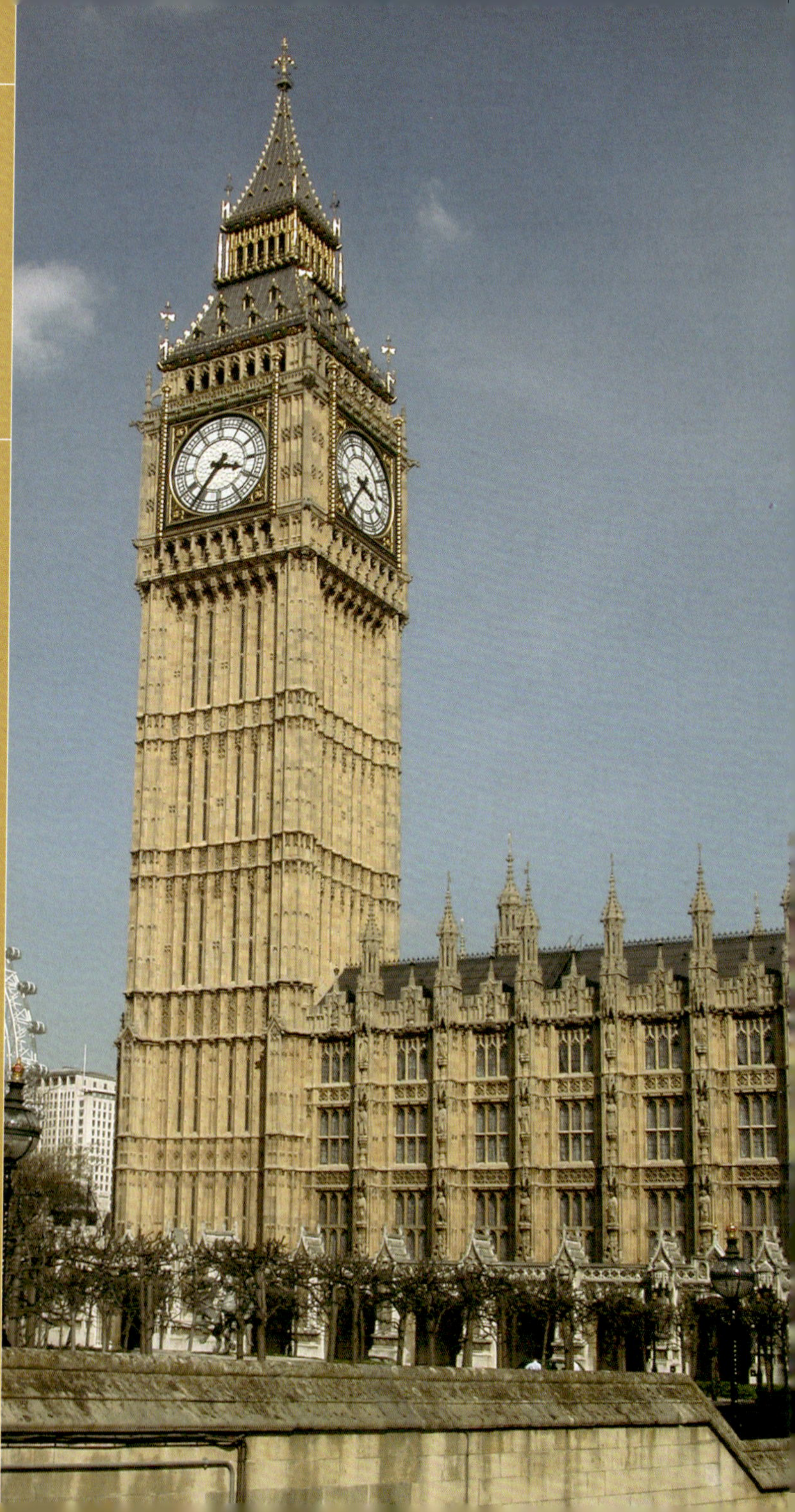

# chapter 2 ▪ "A DESIRE OF DISTINCTION"

**The political rise of Wilberforce was meteoric. At 21, he was first elected to the House of Commons. At 24, his election as Member for Yorkshire helped sway the electoral fortunes of the entire nation. The merchant's son had arrived.**

As the only son of a prosperous family, Wilberforce, as we have seen, was the focus of his mother's and grandfather's dynastic ambitions. His grandfather had twice served as mayor of Hull, and one cousin had become a Member of Parliament. As heir to the substantial wealth and growing influence of a prosperous and respected family, William was expected to take the legacy he would inherit and expand it still further. All of this was true enough, but as a young man of spirit and energy he had come to desire a career in politics for reasons of his own. In the winter of 1780, he often met William Pitt, whom he had known when they were both undergraduates at Cambridge. Their friendship now deepened as they sat together in the gallery of the House of Commons, a place they both were fond of attending.

Wilberforce and Pitt listened with great interest to the debates on the American War of Independence. The fate of nations was being decided in the Commons. In eloquent and historic debates, Lord North, Charles Fox, and Edmund Burke figured prominently. Pitt, as Lord Chatham's son, was opposed to the war — Chatham feared hostilities against America would bring France and Spain into the war. Wilberforce was equally opposed, and this was probably a strong reason

BELOW: Charles Fox, Wilberforce's unlikely ally in the fight to end the slave trade.

27

FACING PAGE: Westminster, the scene of so many important chapters in Wilberforce's life.

why their friendship quickly deepened. They were young men who felt they ought to do their part to put things right.

For several years Wilberforce had been forging friendships with other fellow collegians who aspired to political office. His social gifts, among them his wit and personal warmth, had enabled him to win his way among young men whose social class exceeded his own middle class merchant origins. Since he had been accepted by them, it wasn't unthinkable that he might try to join with his friends as they ran for political office. He rather liked being a part of this exclusive club, and relished the chance to try his wings in the thrust and parry of political debate. These circumstances fueled his ambition because, as he later admitted when looking back on this time of his life, "I was very ambitious."

## Eyes on the Prize

As it happened, Wilberforce would not have to wait long for an election in which to try his chances for a seat in the Commons. A dissolution of Parliament was expected in the summer of 1780, so he began to canvass for the representation of Hull. Politics then, as now, was not a calling for the faint of heart. One story from the hustings in Hull that stayed with Wilberforce for the rest of his life showed just how true this

BELOW: The Wilberforce Memorial Column, Hull, against a night sky in the Victorian era.

## The American War of Independence

The outbreak of the American War in 1775 was described in one British Loyalist song as "The World Turned Upside Down." The Americans in rebellion saw themselves involved in a fight for independence against an oppressive and tyrannical British government. But they were also pitted against loyalist Americans. The conflict was both a rebellion and a civil war.

There were those in England, like Edmund Burke, who sympathized with American grievances and argued for conciliation. Others, like Lord Chatham, opposed the government's policy in prosecuting the war because Britain's great and historic enemy, France, might enter the conflict. This fear was realized. There was, then, a tragic loss of blood and treasure from the great nations of Europe as well as America.

The decisive battle took place at Yorktown in 1781, when forces under the command of Lord Cornwallis surrendered, after a long siege, to a joint force of American and French troops. When the news reached England, Prime Minster Lord North wrote in his diary: "Oh God! It's all over." In September 1783, the Treaty of Paris was signed, officially ending a conflict that had lasted for eight long years.

ABOVE: Winter at Valley Forge, the scene of so many hardships for Washington's army.

was: "When I first canvassed the town, there lived at Hull a fine athletic fellow, by trade a butcher, named Johnny Bell. I rather shrunk from shaking hands with him, saying to one of my staunch supporters that I thought it going rather too low for votes. 'O sir,' was his reply, 'he is a fine fellow if you come to bruising.' The day following the election he came to me privately and said, 'I have found out who threw the stone at you, and I'll kill him tonight.' The threat was seriously intended, and I was forced to repress his zeal by suggesting that it would be too severe a punishment for what had proved, after all, a harmless attempt: 'You must only frighten him,' I said."

Wilberforce's initial canvass of Hull was successful. He then set off for London, where about three hundred Hull voters (with business interests in London) lived in the vicinity of the Thames. He entertained them with suppers in the different public houses of Wapping; speaking to them while the meal and the spirits were in full flow, he gained confidence in public speaking. As the summer advanced, Wilberforce returned to Hull, having every reason to believe that his campaign for one of Hull's two seats in the Commons would succeed. His family ties, growing reputation for eloquence, social gifts, and the liberal use of his wealth in public house entertainments — all of these things were having an effect.

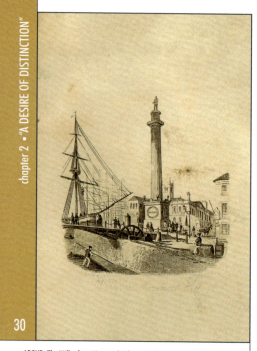

ABOVE: The Wilberforce Memorial Column, Hull, as it appeared in the 1800s.

30

ABOVE: The Wilberforce School for the Blind, circa 1900, established to honor his memory. This charitable institution is now the Wilberforce Trust.

William's growing hopes, however, were almost disappointed by the threat of a hasty dissolution of the sitting Parliament, which would have fixed the day of election before his 21st birthday, and thus make him ineligible to stand. It was with great relief that he learned that the session would survive his birthday. When his birthday came, voters who had yet to be convinced of Wilberforce's virtues as a candidate were treated to a feast in which an ox was roasted whole in one of his fields.

The day lingered long in the memory of those who attended the feast. Forty-seven years later, on the last tour of Yorkshire that he ever took, Wilberforce stopped at Huddersfield. There he was approached by an old man named Smart — "an honest, warm-hearted shopkeeper, originally from Hull." Wilberforce recalled: "He knew me when he was himself a boy — remembered the ox roasted whole, &c., and the joke about my dear sister." The joke, a fine old chestnut, was this: During this first campaign, Wilberforce and his sister Sarah, whom the family called Sally, appeared at the window of the High Street mansion in which he was born to give a brief speech to the crowd that had assembled there. Someone in the enthusiastic throng shouted "Mr. Wilberforce and Miss Wilberforce

ABOVE: A color engraving of the Wilberforce House, Hull, about 1850.

31

for ever!" Without missing a beat, Sally stepped forward and shouted back: "Not Miss Wilberforce for ever, I hope."

By mid-September 1780, Wilberforce found himself in a sharp election contest. He faced three formidable tasks: overcoming the interest of Lord Rockingham, the most powerful nobleman in the county; challenging the political influence of Sir George Savile, Yorkshire's wealthy and respected representative; and opposing candidates supported by the government of Lord North, the influence of which was particularly strong in Hull. For his part, Wilberforce was barely 21. In opposition to the substantial interests set against him, he could offer an independent character and the not inconsiderable influence of his family. He also drew upon his natural eloquence and his own substantial wealth, spending between £8,000 and £9,000 (around one million dollars today) over the course of the contest.

The motto of the day for aspiring political candidates might well have been "Line their pockets, and their hearts and minds will follow." Wilberforce had no scruple about following the long established custom of bribery. The single vote of a resident elector could be purchased for two guineas; four were paid for what was called "a plumper"; and the expenses of a

ABOVE: The Rotunda, Ranelagh Gardens. Wilberforce often walked here with fashionable friends.

freeman's journey from London averaged £10 ($1,200 today) a piece. Technically, such payments were not illegal — that is to say the letter of the law was not broken — because the money was not paid until the last day on which election petitions could be presented.

Against all expectation, Wilberforce, the political novice, carried the day against the powerful interests he opposed. In fact, such was his command of the electorate that his tally at the poll numbered exactly the same as that of his two fellow candidates combined.

| Lord Robert Manners | 673 |
|---|---|
| David Hartley | 453 |
| William Wilberforce | 1,126 |

The merchant's son had arrived. Added to his electoral success, important friendships like the one he shared with William Pitt provided an entrance into the highest social circles. Wilberforce's obvious social gifts took care of the rest. He was adept at witty sayings, possessed a very fine singing voice and had great natural charm. These drawing room accomplishments were more or less in service to his ambition. "Distinction," he wrote, "was my darling object."

## "To Be Young Was Very Heaven"

Wilberforce and Pitt became brothers-in-arms, and as close as brothers. Though both were politically independent, lending their allegiance to none of the recognized party chiefs of the day, they shared a common antipathy to the war with America. Both spoke out against it, and Wilberforce's use of invective during his speeches early in 1782 helped bring down Lord North's government. He could mimic North to perfection, and the tactics of ridicule were a potent weapon in his rhetorical arsenal. He used them repeatedly in attacking the "old fat fellow," as he called North.

Aside from what they had in common politically, Wilberforce and Pitt were part of the same set of friends. The group numbered roughly 25 and was for the most part made up of young men who had passed through Cambridge together and entered public life at the same time. Their favorite haunt was a club called Goostree's. Pitt practically lived there, eating his evening meal there every night during one winter.

BELOW: The Victorian-era memorial to Wilberforce and the Anti-Slavery Society.

BELOW: Wilberforce as a young MP. A political prodigy, he was elected to the Commons at the age of 21.

*liam Wilberforce Esq.r M.P.*

*Nature imprints upon whate'er we see.*

Wilberforce was still fond of gambling. Diary entries from this period record more than once the loss of £100 (almost $12,000 today) at the faro table. However, he gave up gambling after one evening's game in which he rose the winner of £600 ($72,000 today.) The friends with whom he had been playing were only heirs to future fortunes, whereas Wilberforce already had his, and they could not meet such a debt without great inconvenience. No doubt his friendships among his set deepened when his friends learned that he had no heart to fleece them.

Wilberforce did, however, feel no reluctance whatsoever about taking on the government of Lord North and the war against America that he felt was so ruinous for Britain. In a speech given on February 22, 1782, Wilberforce let fly at North with everything he had. He declared that "while the present ministry existed, there were no prospects of either peace or happiness" for Britain. To underscore the point that North and his administration had to resign, he called them "furious madmen" who had pursued "the ruinous war" against America in a "cruel, bloody, impracticable manner."

North resigned as prime minister in March 1782 and Wilberforce's role in ending his tenure had not gone unnoticed. The opposition party under Lord Rockingham now came into power. Ending the war with America had been their rallying cry, and Wilberforce's services in helping to bring down North — though Wilberforce was not a member of Rockingham's party — gave rise to a series of rumors that showed how greatly Rockingham and his partisans valued what he had done. Wilberforce's sons wrote: "So prevalent was the idea that he was to be included in the new official arrangements, and raised to the Upper House, that he received various applications for the supply of his robes upon that occasion." All

ABOVE: Benjamin Franklin, the American founding father who greeted Wilberforce warmly in 1783, and who shared Wilberforce's antipathy toward the slave trade.

## William Pitt (1759–1806)

Groomed for greatness from boyhood by his father, Lord Chatham, William Pitt was both the youngest prime minister in British history and one of Britain's most gifted politicians. He possessed a keen intellect and commanding presence. He could also summon a powerful and persuasive eloquence.

Wilberforce always said that Pitt's great ambition was to be a peace-minister, to champion causes like parliamentary reform, to restore Britain's finances after the disastrous American war, and to end great evils like the slave trade. It was not to be. In February 1793, just ten years after the Treaty of Paris, France declared war on Britain. A final end to the fight against France was not to come until the Battle of Waterloo in 1815. It was then that an alliance, led by British forces under the Duke of Wellington, defeated Napoleon.

Pitt had not lived to see it. He had died early in 1806, shortly after receiving the awful news of Napoleon's destruction of the armies of Russia and Austria at Austerlitz. At the request of Pitt's family, Wilberforce carried the family banner before the funeral cortege. It was one last tribute to a friend with whom he had been as close as a brother. Pitt has come down to us in history as a cold and aloof character — political in every fiber of his being. Wilberforce knew a different man — one who was naturally rather shy, but when among his intimate friends, as animated as anyone could be. Wilberforce recalled, "He was the wittiest man I ever knew."

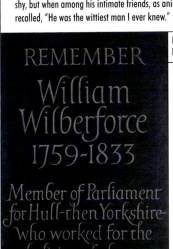

LEFT: The Wilberforce Memorial plaque in York Minster. It pays tribute to his legacy with simple eloquence: "Remember William Wilberforce."

of which meant that Wilberforce was to be given office in the Rockingham administration, raised to the peerage, and to take a seat in the House of Lords. He was not yet 23. The death of Lord Rockingham in July 1782 ended these hopes but in no way detracted from the idea that the able and ambitious young man was someone to keep your eye on — and to watch your back should you cross swords with him.

In the autumn of 1783, Wilberforce and Pitt decided to travel to France and they were soon regular guests at the court of Louis XVI and Marie Antoinette; they were fascinated by what they saw. Wilberforce received a hearty greeting from Benjamin Franklin as "a rising member of the English Parliament who had opposed the war with America." He also met the Marquis de Lafayette, with whom he would later have important dealings. It was a heady time and he revelled in it.

## A Fool's Errand

The notion that he had arrived socially and politically encouraged Wilberforce to conceive what in 1784 must have appeared to everyone but himself "a mad scheme." On December 19, 1783, a new administration of the Fox-North Coalition ended and Pitt became prime minister at the age of 24. His fledgling government was seen as "a mince-pie administration," and needed shoring up. A general election was decided upon in hopes that enough new members would be returned to strengthen Pitt's mandate to govern. It was then that Wilberforce decided to seek election as one of two Members of Parliament for the entire county of Yorkshire — one of the most powerful elected seats in the government. Against him were arrayed the landed aristocrats for whom the county was little more than a fiefdom. Wilberforce was also directly challenging the partisans of Charles Fox. He attacked Fox and "his vile coalition" with great vehemence. Wilberforce was also

BELOW: The House of Commons in the early years of Wilberforce's career. (William Pitt addressing the House of Commons on the French Declaration of War, 1793, by Karl Anton Hickel.)

ABOVE: An aerial view of the Houses of Parliament and Westminster Abbey.

strongly opposed to the way Britain was governing India with "violence and corruption."

In the first parliamentary session of 1784, Wilberforce continued his attacks on the Fox-North coalition relentlessly. In speech after speech he brought caustic accusations against them, saying they "had sacrificed every principle of honor," that they were bent on "annihilating the prerogative of the crown" and the balance of the constitution. Wilberforce's withering attacks led Fox to hate him for a time. Even Pitt, though grateful on one level that Wilberforce was "tearing the enemy to pieces," felt it necessary for a time to call Wilberforce off. Wilberforce himself later described the mindset that led him to act as he had done toward Lord North and Fox: "Party creates and diffuses a false moral system, it . . . provides an amnesty for every crime. Staunch zeal for the party excuses all, defends all . . . and justifies all." In the end, Wilberforce's denunciations of Fox, in concert with a genuine desire for political reform, carried the day against all expectation. His victory was complete and so decisive that candidates on the side of Pitt throughout the nation traced their success to Wilberforce's lead. From Down Street, Pitt wrote: "I cannot congratulate you enough on your glorious success."

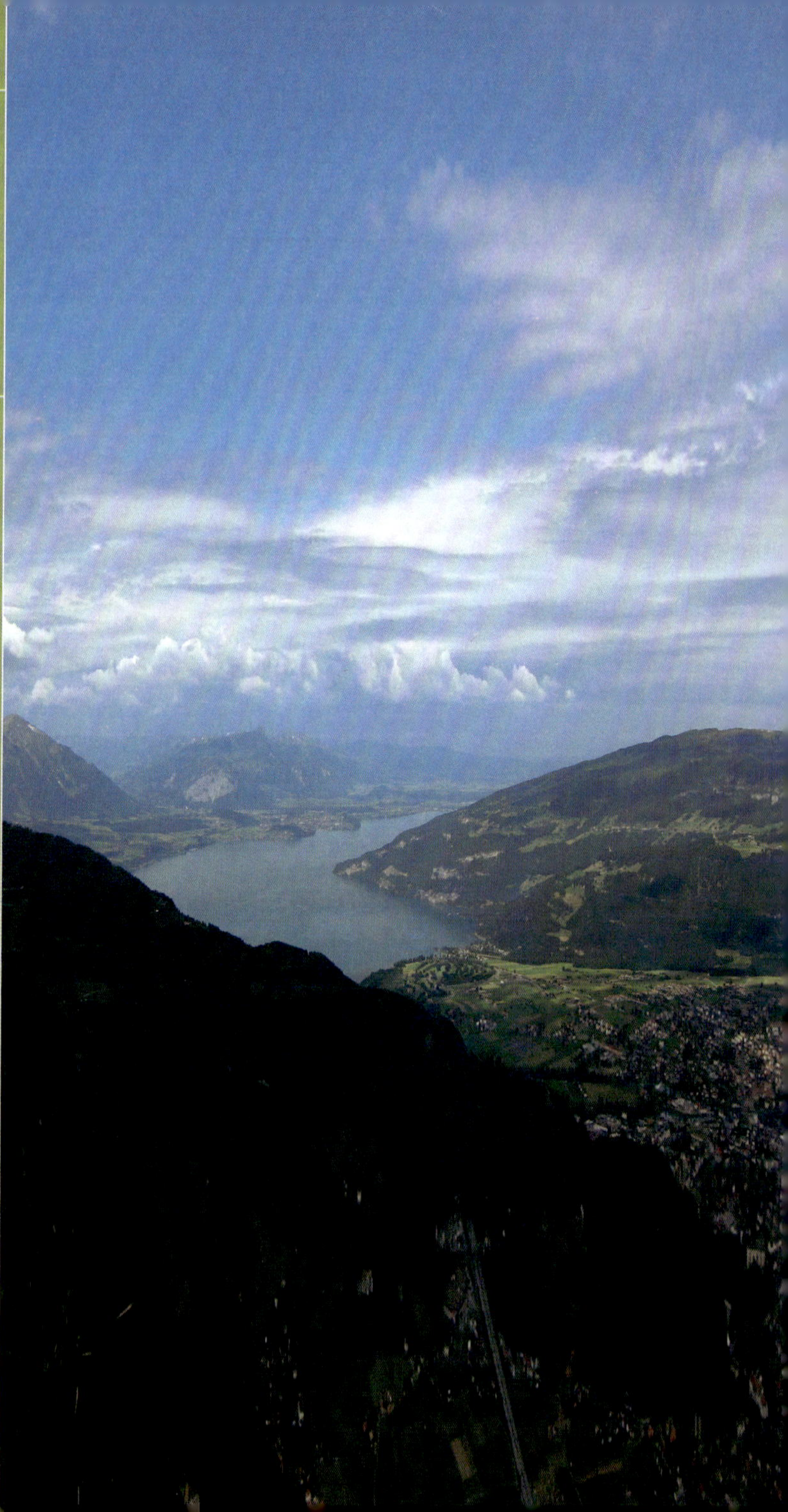

# chapter 3 ■ THE GRAND CHANGE

**Wilberforce's political star had reached unexpected heights, yet the future that lay before him was nothing like what he or most others expected. The entire course of his life was about to be re-directed. Britain and the world would never be the same.**

Wilberforce promptly decided to take a continental tour to savor his parliamentary victory. Lasting from the autumn of 1784 through to the autumn of the following year, he stayed with the fashionable set at Nice, was transfixed by the paradise of Interlaken, and traveled through Italy. In spite of all of this, however, he returned to England a decidedly different man. He was, in fact, in the throes of a spiritual crisis.

Things started none too promisingly. Wilberforce wanted his cultured, entertaining friend Dr. William Burgh to accompany him. All the ladies in the party (his mother, sister, and cousin Bessy Smith) would be traveling together in one carriage. Riding with them was not an option he relished. Burgh would be just the sort of person he needed as a companion. Burgh, however, was unable to go, and the start of the tour was fast approaching.

Quite by chance Wilberforce met up with his former tutor at Hull Grammar School, Isaac Milner. Milner had moved from Hull to Cambridge where he was quickly elected a Fellow of the Royal Society. Yet he was still the friend from Hull that

Wilberforce remembered — "lively and dashing in his conversation." He was a great bear of a man with a booming voice.

On impulse, Wilberforce asked Milner to join him. Milner agreed, but before the evening was over, William had cause to regret his impulsive invitation. While the two men were dining, the conversation turned to a particular evangelical vicar.

"He's a good man," Wilberforce said, "but one who carries things too far."

"Not a bit too far, I think," said Milner.

"This declaration greatly surprised me," Wilberforce recalled: "Had I known at first what his opinions were, it would have decided me against making the offer." However, the invitation had been given and Wilberforce's pride would not let him withdraw it.

### The Skeptic's Progress

As the party set out for Calais, Wilberforce continued to "let loose my sceptical opinions, or treat . . . with ridicule the principles of vital religion." Milner replied, "Wilberforce, I don't pretend to be a match for you in this sort of running fire; but if you really wish to discuss them in a serious and argumentative manner, I shall be most happy to enter on them with you." For some years, Wilberforce had been attending Theophilus Lindsey's Unitarian Chapel on Essex Street in London. Lindsey worshiped a benevolent Providence, a being who was in some way also the judge of man's actions; but he rejected Christ, the Trinity, the Christian view of the atonement, and the authority of Scripture. Wilberforce went to Lindsey's

BELOW: Philip Doddridge, whose book, *The Rise and Progress of Religion in the Soul,* challenged Wilberforce's ideas about Christianity.

40

ABOVE: The tomb of Isaac Watts in Bunhill Fields burial ground, London. It was he who suggested to Philip Doddridge the plan for his book.

chapel "not from any particular preference for his doctrines . . . but because he seemed more earnest and practical than others." He was now wholly against the faith of his uncle and aunt in Wimbledon. But here he was, facing the prospect of a long tour with Milner, someone whose views — he had discovered too late — were precisely those he was trying to avoid!

Thinking he could easily poke holes in Milner's religious views or at least enjoy a spirited debate, Wilberforce agreed to discuss these matters of faith. He soon discovered he had more on his hands than he bargained for. Milner understood the intellectual heart of Christianity, could articulate its beliefs in a winsome and compelling manner, and backed his answers with the Bible. William found himself unable lightly to dismiss Milner's position.

More compelling still was a book they agreed to read together, *The Rise and Progress of Religion in the Soul*, by Philip Doddridge. This classic work has been described as "a reasoned, elegant exposition" of Christianity. Wilberforce had seen it lying on a table in one of the inns where the party stopped for the night. Apparently, Bessy Smith had brought it along. He picked it up and asked Milner, "What do you think of this?" Milner replied, "It's one of the best books ever written. Let's take it with us and read it on our journey." This book, which so affected Wilberforce and many others before and since, was really a guided tour of the process of conversion.

Wilberforce and Milner had to return to England briefly, but rejoined the traveling party in July 1785, going by

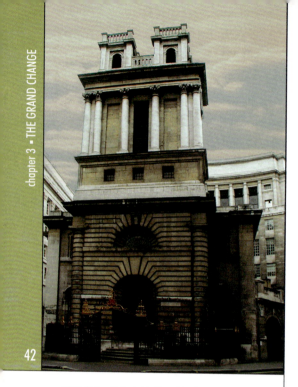

ABOVE: St. Mary Woolnoth, John Newton's London Church, as it is today.

way of Switzerland. There, at Interlaken, "a vast garden of the loveliest fertility and beauty stretched out at the base of the giant Alps," the two friends resumed the subject of religion. Their conversations became deeply important, as they read the Greek New Testament and closely examined its doctrines. The two were so often lost in discussion that the ladies began to complain that visits were no longer being made to their carriage. As Wilberforce recalled, everything that Milner said "tended to increase my attention to religion." He continued to press on Milner his doubts, objections, and difficulties, but gradually his mind began to change, even though his heart remained unmoved.

Returning home in October 1785, Wilberforce struggled with what it meant to embrace the Christian life. He wrote in his diary for one day: "The deep guilt and black ingratitude of my past life forced itself upon me in the strongest colors, and I condemned myself for having wasted my precious time, and opportunities, and talents." He longed to find peace with God, and now knew that it could only come through Christ. He struggled to reconcile his emerging faith with his understanding of service in political life.

William considered giving up politics and being ordained into the church, but he could not see his way forward clearly. Finally, he decided to call on John Newton, the man he had so admired in boyhood, and yet he was wary, his whole career was at stake. On December 2, 1785, he delivered a sealed letter to Newton at his London church, St. Mary Woolnoth.

Sir,

There is no need of apology for intruding on you, when the errand is religion. I wish to have some serious conversation with you . . . the earlier the more agreeable to me. I have had ten thousand doubts within myself, whether or not I should discover myself to you; but every argument against doing it has its foundation in pride. I am sure you will hold yourself bound to let no one living know of this application, or of my visit, till I release you from the obligation. . . . P.S. Remember that I must be secret, and that the gallery of the House is now so universally attended, that the face of a member of Parliament is pretty well known.

## Crossing the Rubicon

The following Wednesday was named for Wilberforce to visit

BELOW: Charles Square as it is today. The red-brick home, center image, is very like Newton's home, which was immediately to the right.

BELOW: The closing salutation from one of Wilberforce's letters. "I am ever, my dear Sir, affectionately & sincerely yours, W. Wilberforce."

43

Newton at his home in Charles Square. Still Wilberforce was struggling. Something about going to Newton represented a sort of spiritual Rubicon to him. He walked around the square once, then again, trying to decide whether or not to knock on the door. Finally he did and the two men had a lengthy conversation. Newton told William that he had never ceased to pray for him or believe that someday he would return to his boyhood faith. "When I came away," Wilberforce wrote, "I

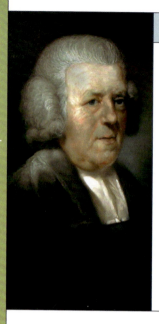

## John Newton

John Newton was once a slave trader himself, but after his conversion to evangelical Christianity, he published his story, *An Authentic Narrative*, in 1764. He is also the author of many hymns, including the timeless "Amazing Grace." The literary impact of *An Authentic Narrative* was such that many critics have seen Newton "as anticipating William Blake's prophetic vision, as a source for Coleridge's *Rime of the Ancient Mariner*, and for episodes in Wordsworth's *Prelude*."

The *Authentic Narrative* went through ten British and eight American editions before 1800. It was quickly translated into several other languages. Among many others, it had a deep effect on both Wilberforce and Lord Dartmouth, the founder of Dartmouth College in America. Newton was a spiritual advisor to both, and he set Wilberforce on the path to leading the 20-year struggle that ultimately ended the British slave trade.

Newton lived just long enough to see the end of the slave trade in 1807, even as Wilberforce himself lived just long enough to see the end of slavery throughout the British Empire in 1833.

found my mind in a calm, tranquil state, more humbled, and looking more devoutly up to God."

Newton, who had known so many storms in life, helped Wilberforce to understand that one could serve Christ in the political arena; in subsequent meetings, Newton gave William the examples of Daniel, Joseph, and other Old Testament leaders. Newton and another minister, Thomas Scott, countered the advice of others who had urged Wilberforce to retire from public life completely. John Newton also encouraged Wilberforce when he occasionally grew despondent. Over time, Wilberforce found his feet spiritually. By Easter 1786, what he later came to call his "grand change" was complete: "By degrees, the promises and offers of the gospel produced in me something of a settled peace of conscience. I devoted myself for whatever might be the term of my future life, to the service of my God and Saviour."

Newton continued to watch William's progress. At Easter 1786, he wrote to his friend, the poet William Cowper: "I judge he is now decidedly on the right track . . . I hope the Lord will make him a blessing both as a Christian and a statesman. How seldom do these characters coincide! But they are not incompatible." To Wilberforce, he wrote at the end of the year: "I hope that great usefulness to the public, and in the church of God, will be your present reward."

At the same time that he planned to seek counsel from Newton, Wilberforce thought it important to share what had been happening in his life with Pitt, in many respects his closest friend. Wilberforce did this before he met with John Newton, and he was not sure whether he ought to remain in politics, or if he did, what impact his great change might have on his friendship with the prime minister. He had to warn Pitt that from now on, Pitt would not always be able to rely on his political support.

It was the classic preamble to a new convert saying he wished to make something of a clean break with the past. That this was so is confirmed by Wilberforce's response to the letter he received from Pitt: "On the 2nd of December, I got Pitt's answer. It was full of kindness — nothing I had told him, he said, could affect our friendship; that he wished me always to act as I thought right." Pitt's feelings on that day in Wimbledon must have run close to what he shared in his letter to Wilberforce. That letter has survived, providing a close view of all that transpired between these two great friends. It is an extraordinary letter, written from 10 Downing Street on December 2, 1785, and addressed to "My dear Wilberforce."

Pitt began by expressing his strong regard for his friend, and that his happiness was as important as his own; if they ever had

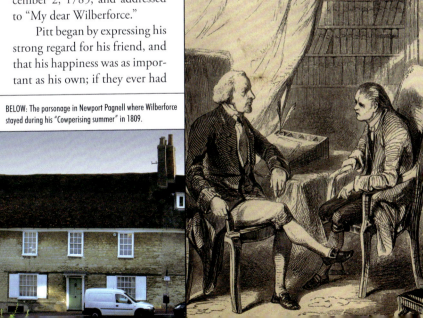

BELOW: Depiction of Wilberforce's December 1785 interview with Newton, from American Mary Collier's 1855 biography of Wilberforce.

BELOW: The parsonage in Newport Pagnell where Wilberforce stayed during his "Cowperising summer" in 1809.

to differ, it would make no difference to their friendship. Pitt expressed his fear that William had been seriously misled in his plans to withdraw from public life altogether — and now he set out to change his friend's mind:

ABOVE: William Cowper, Wilberforce's favorite poet.

ABOVE: Thomas Scott, noted biblical commentator and author of the classic treatise *The Force of Truth*.

But forgive me if I cannot help expressing my fear that you are nevertheless deluding yourself into principles which have but too much tendency to counteract your own object, and to render your virtues and your talents useless both to yourself and mankind. . . . If a Christian may act in the several relations of life, must he seclude himself from them all to become so?

Surely the principles as well as the practice of Christianity are simple, and lead not to meditation only but to action. . . . What I would ask of you, as a mark both of your friendship and of the candour which belongs to your mind, is to open yourself fully and without reserve to one, who, believe me, does not know how to separate your happiness from his own.

You do not explain either the degree or the duration of the retirement which you have prescribed to yourself. . . . I am sure you will not wonder if I am inquisitive on such a subject. The only way in which you can satisfy me is by conversation. There ought to be no awkwardness or embarrassment to either of us . . . tho' I shall venture to state to you fairly the points where I fear we may differ. . . .

Name any hour at which I can call upon you tomorrow. I am going into Kent, and can take Wimbledon in my way. Reflect, I beg of you, that no principles are the worse for being discussed, and believe me that at all events the full knowledge of the nature and extent of your opinions and intentions will be to me a lasting satisfaction.

Believe me, affectionately and unalterably yours,
W. Pitt

## Two Hours with William Pitt

The two agreed to meet the next morning. The prime minister was convinced that these were temporary feelings that a good conversation would soon dispel. The two friends met at Lauriston House, Wilberforce's Wimbledon villa. One can picture them, sitting before a fire in Wilberforce's drawing room, in serious conversation. It was a moment such as rarely happens in history, a prime minister setting all else aside — the business of state and pressing appointments — to be with his friend, even though that friend was not sure if he would be able to continue with him in politics. They talked for nearly two hours. "I opened myself completely to him," Wilberforce

ABOVE: Scene from Cowper's epic poem, *The Task*, Wilberforce's favorite poem.

remembered. "I admitted that as far as I could conform to the world, with a perfect regard to my duty to God, myself, and my fellow-creatures, I was bound to do it."

In retrospect, Wilberforce's interview with Pitt was profoundly important. Taking place, as it did, just before his first crucial meeting with Newton, Pitt's letter and his interview with Wilberforce helped to set the stage for the meeting with Newton.

Pitt and Wilberforce seemed to have reached something of a stalemate. Their friendship for one another remained unaltered, yet something had changed. Pitt, Wilberforce recalled, "tried to reason me out of my convictions, but soon found himself unable to combat their correctness, if Christianity were true." Wilberforce's faith had stood the test, but Pitt had helped him to see it in a new light. Wilberforce would have to rethink his idea of withdrawing from public office. For the moment, Wilberforce would take no action about his political future.

BELOW: Village sign for Olney, the home of Newton and Cowper

When Wilberforce went to Newton, he could now tell him all that had taken place. Newton was just the person for Wilberforce to have sought out. Newton, Scott, and Pitt had all helped him to see, though for different reasons, that his was a calling to service in political life. In time, as he said, he found "a settled peace of conscience." He would now do his best to serve as a Christian statesman, though it was a thing for which he had no sure pattern.

The transformation was remarkable. Renouncing the win-at-all-costs politics of hostility and vehemence, he came to

ABOVE: The Church of St. Peter and St. Paul, Olney, the church of Cowper and Newton, before Newton moved to St. Mary Woolnoth in London, also the scene of so many pleasant associations for Wilberforce.

exhibit what many contemporaries — even political opponents — called a good faith; they saw eventually that good intent was more than words, it was proved real through actions. Wilberforce set about mending broken relationships, such as the one with Charles Fox, Pitt's great parliamentary opponent in the Commons. Over time, Wilberforce's life came to exemplify a civility that had been glaringly absent from his earlier political conduct. The course of his life was forever altered. Francis Bacon, the 16th century essayist whom Wilberforce much admired, once commented, "It is a sad fate for a man to die too well known to everybody else, and still unknown to himself." Wilberforce had found his rest and peace with God.

Looking back on it all many years later he wrote, "Surely when I think of the way in which I went on for many years — from about [the age of] sixteen to 1785–6, I can only fall down with astonishment . . . before the throne of grace and adore with wonder . . . that infinite mercy of God which did not cast me off; but on the contrary, guiding me by a way which I knew not, led me to those from whom I was to receive the knowledge of."

SAINT
NICHOLAS

BEFORE · MY · FATHER · WHICH · IS · IN · HEAVEN

The Lord thy God will turn thy captivity and have compassion upon thee

# chapter 4 ■ SUPPRESSING THE SLAVE TRADE

**Against a backdrop of world war, and with sterling perseverance, Wilberforce and his colleagues stood firm in their resolve to end the slave trade. His own path during these years was to prove more difficult and trying than he could have ever imagined.**

During the 1790s, Britain fought for her very existence. Not until Napoleon's defeat at Waterloo in 1815 was there close to what Wilberforce called the "catastrophe of the twenty-five years drama since 1789." Yet it was then, when the threat of a French invasion was ever-present, that his most important reforms were achieved. He would endure the near severing of vital friendships, debilitating bouts of illness, death threats, and crushing legislative defeats.

The fall of the Bastille on July 14, 1789, marked the close of the "old regime" in France. At first, the changes across the Channel were not viewed with alarm. Wilberforce, along with many others, read Burke's perceptive *Reflections on the Revolution in France* when it was published in November 1790, but as yet events had not confirmed the fears Burke expressed. However, by 1792 the reign of terror under Robespierre began. In February 1793, France declared war on Britain. It was devastating, but by this time Wilberforce had already weathered several serious storms.

## Two Great Objects
Wilberforce had taken up the great work of his life on Sunday,

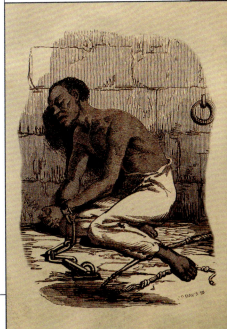

ABOVE: A 19th-century engraving depicting the horrors of the slave trade.

51

FACING PAGE: The Wilberforce window at the Holy Trinity Church, Clapham, which commemorates Wilberforce's legacy as the leader of the 20-year fight to abolish the slave trade.

October 28, 1787. On that day, he had met with John Newton. The two friends talked for a long time and discussed the great needs that existed in Britain and the evils of the slave trade, which Wilberforce had been discussing for some time with friends like Thomas Clarkson, Sir Charles and Lady Middleton, and James Ramsay. Wilberforce now saw his path clearly. After Newton left, he wrote in his diary: "God has set before me two great objects, the suppression of the slave trade and the reformation of manners [i.e., morals]."

Wilberforce now called for the abolition of the slave trade, which Pitt had also urged him to do during an earnest discussion under a great oak on Pitt's estate in Kent. Wilberforce became immersed in research — sometimes for 14 hours a day. However, by early 1788 something was wrong. His diary now contained frequent entries of "indifferent health," or "very unwell." His condition worsened and the result of consultations were not encouraging: "Entire decay of all the vital functions. He has not stamina to last a fortnight." His physicians urged him to journey to Bath, thinking the mineral waters might prolong his life.

Just before setting out, Wilberforce asked Pitt to undertake the cause of abolition in the event of his death. He wrote afterward: "Pitt, with a warmth of principle and friendship that have made me love him better than I ever did before, has taken on himself the management of the business."

## James Ramsay (1733–1789)

James Ramsay entered the navy in 1757, but when an injury disqualified him from further service, he became a vicar in the Church of England and settled on the Caribbean island of St. Kitts. Along with his pastoral duties, Ramsay practiced medicine. He welcomed everyone, black and white, strongly criticized the cruel treatment of slaves, and began many measures to improve their condition.

He soon came under attack from the planters and, exhausted by the conflict, he returned to Britain, taking with him his servant and friend, a former slave called Nestor. Ramsay became vicar of Teston and Nettlestead in Kent, where his loving and gentle nature endeared him to his parishioners. In 1784, he published his *Essay on the Treatment . . . of Slaves in the British Sugar Colonies*. It documented the horrors associated with slavery and the slave trade. Despite his failing health, he strongly supported Wilberforce in the slavery cause.

ABOVE: Barham Court, Teston, overlooking the Medway valley, southwest of Maidstone, Kent. Here Wilberforce had early consultations with those who sought to end the slave trade.

Wilberforce reached Bath in grave extremity. As a last resort, his physicians prescribed medicinal doses of opium and, though not providing a cure for what appears to have been ulcerative colitis, it turned the tide. Yet even as his physical reserves were replenished, he began to suffer hallucinations — probably the result of the opium. This, combined with the lingering effects of the overwork and stress that initially induced his illness, brought on torments of the mind and spirit that subsided only gradually. Continued rest, prayer, and the kind attention of friends helped to bring Wilberforce back to himself.

Meanwhile, Pitt moved a resolution binding the House of Commons to consider the circumstances of the slave trade. A warm debate followed, and the expressed opinion of the House seemed strongly in support of abolition. Edmund Burke declared himself a staunch opponent of the trade. Charles Fox stated that he "had almost made up his mind to immediate abolition," and here was

ABOVE: Memorial plaque for James Ramsay on the wall of the church he pastored in Teston, the Church of St. Peter and St. Paul.

## Edmund Burke (1729–1797)

BELOW: Edmund Burke, Wilberforce's celebrated contemporary and good friend.

Edmund Burke was a great statesman, orator, and author, and it was he who predicted that the French Revolution would ultimately end in a despotic reign of terror. His political writings are known the world over.

Far less known is the support that came to Burke in the final troubled days of his life. In early April 1797, Wilberforce published his *Practical View of Christianity*. Its winsome and compelling arguments had a profound influence, and it became "the manifesto of the evangelical movement."

Wilberforce could recall no more touching instance of his book's reception than what it meant to Burke in the two last days of his life. Near the end, Burke summoned his doctor and committed a message to him: "Tell Wilberforce that I have derived much comfort from it, and that if I live I will thank him for having sent such a book into the world."

seen one important result of Wilberforce's great change. Repenting of his earlier treatment of Fox, Wilberforce had worked to restore their friendship. Differences still persisted, but both men now found common ground where they could. Ending the slave trade was something both were committed to. Throughout the summer and autumn of 1788 Wilberforce continued his long convalescence.

## The Opening Round Against the Slave Trade

Wilberforce returned to Parliament early in 1789. On May 12 he gave a powerful speech which lasted three hours. Edmund Burke declared that Wilberforce had "brought forward the subject in a manner the most masterly, impressive, and eloquent . . . it equalled any thing he had heard in modern times, and was not perhaps to be surpassed in the remains of Grecian eloquence."

Wilberforce spoke of the transportation of the slaves to the West Indies — the infamous Middle Passage: "So much misery, condensed in so little room, is more than the human imagination had ever before conceived." Wilberforce insisted that: "A trade founded in iniquity, and carried on, as this was, must be abolished, let the policy be what it might — let the consequences be what they would." Wilberforce argued that he could not believe God would make plunder and bloodshed

ABOVE: The Pump Room, Bath, as it would have appeared in Wilberforce's time.

BELOW: Sir Charles Middleton, Lord Barham. He and his wife, Lady Margaret, were instrumental in Wilberforce's decision to lead the fight to end the slave trade.

necessary to the well-being of any part of His universe. He based his arguments upon "the dictates of his conscience, the principles of justice, the laws of religion, and of God." Finally he declared, "This House must decide, and must justify to all the world, and to their own consciences" the morality and principles of their decision: "Let us make reparation to Africa."

Despite his eloquence, and staunch support from Pitt and Burke, the Commons decided that they needed to hear more evidence. It was a delaying tactic used often in the years ahead.

## Defeat, Delay, and a Duel

In April 1791, serious debate finally commenced. In a speech lasting nearly four hours, Wilberforce opened "the hidden things of darkness . . . exposing the horrific traffic in its native deformity." Colonel Banastre Tarleton, a hero of the war with America and a violent supporter of the slave trade, who had once boasted of having killed more men than anyone living, tried to distract Wilberforce, but he was as firm as a rock. From time to time "when Wilberforce had drawn a particularly strong inference or conclusion . . . Pitt held up his hands in admiration." Repeatedly during the speech the cry of "Hear him! Hear him!" echoed throughout the House. Wilberforce's voice "seemed to strengthen as he went on."

In the end it was all for nothing; 88 members voted for abolition, 163 against. In 1792 things improved. Wilberforce's masterly presentation of dramatic evidence, and one of Pitt's greatest speeches, brought the Commons to the brink of ending the slave trade. But at a crucial point, Henry Dundas — a supporter of the trade — rose and called for moderation. He suggested the insertion of the word "gradual" into the bill. This rescued supporters of the trade just when the vote would have gone Wilberforce's way. Those nervous about Wilberforce's call for immediate abolition could throw their support to this more appealing amendment. Gradual abolition was approved. At first Wilberforce was despondent: "I cannot help regretting we have been able to do no more." Further reflection lifted his spirits: "On the whole this is more than I expected two months ago, and I have much cause for thankfulness."

His old mentor, Isaac Milner, wrote to

BELOW: Thomas Clarkson's dramatic depiction of the hold of the slave ship *Brookes*. One of the most enduring images of the abolition struggle.

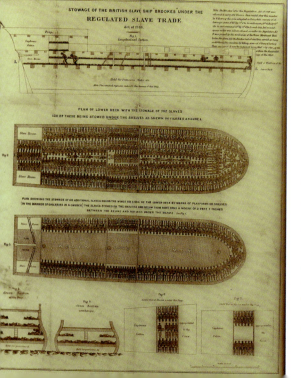

ABOVE: The kind of horrific cruelty Wilberforce described to the House of Commons during debates on the slave trade.

57

William, reminding him that years earlier he had declared that if Wilberforce succeeded on this issue, his would be a life spent far better that being prime minister for many years.

Within weeks, Wilberforce confronted a more severe threat — a challenge to a duel from a slave ship captain named Rolleston. Wilberforce was no coward, he had already faced murderous threats from another slaver named Robert Norris and still remained unmoved in his determination to end the slave trade — but he was opposed to dueling on clear Christian principles. In the event nothing further transpired, and as quickly as he had appeared, the shadowy figure of Rolleston faded away.

More threats of violence, however, were to follow. In the recently concluded slave trade debate of April 2, Wilberforce had been repeatedly pressed by the House to name the slave ship captain whose murder of a young Negro girl of 15 he had described. "Name, name!" was shouted. Wilberforce at last revealed it — Captain John Kimber.

Kimber was arrested and tried for murder, but acquitted because the Admiralty judge "identified himself with the prisoner's cause." Kimber demanded "a public apology, £5,000 [$560,000 today], and such a place under government as would

ABOVE: Beilby Porteus, the abolitionist Bishop of London who was one of Wilberforce's staunchest supporters.

make me comfortable." After consulting with Pitt, Wilberforce penned a brief refusal. Kimber began lying in wait for him and the threat was so real that Lord Rokeby, Wilberforce's friend, became his armed companion on a journey into Yorkshire. Two years of menacing threats followed, ended only by the interference of Lord Sheffield — who apparently had some influence over Kimber.

## War with France — and with the Prime Minister!

Even as Kimber faded away, other events caused concern. By December 1794, Wilberforce had come to have grave doubts about the course of the war with France. He was not a pacifist, believing that the Bible allowed for defensive wars of which this was one, since France had declared war on Britain. However, he saw himself "as a member of the British parliament, on whom it was peculiarly incumbent to take care that the blood and treasure of this country were not wantonly sacrificed." He believed Pitt was too warlike and the best course was to try for peace. Wilberforce knew this would be fragile, but the outcome of war would not be better.

Wilberforce knew his opposition could force a crisis of confidence that could bring down Pitt's government. However he looked at it, his choices were difficult and painful. After his great change, Wilberforce had assured Pitt that he would always remain true to his conscience, but he never foresaw this. With a heavy heart, he urged negotiations toward peace, "upon just and reasonable terms," but concluded that if this proved impossible because of the "violence and ambition of the enemy," then the alternative would be a just and necessary war.

It was a principled amendment. Nowhere did Wilberforce accuse those with whom he disagreed of being warmongers. He mentioned no one by name, and declared it "a painful act of duty in expressing his dissent," having to differ "with those with whom it had been the happiness of his political life so generally to agree."

Wilberforce's speech made a deep impression, although it produced a storm of criticism and nearly severed his friendship with Pitt. The prime minister was unable to sleep following Wilberforce's motion. When a party of their mutual friends met soon after, Wilberforce was conspicuously absent; he knew he was not wanted there: "I felt all day out of spirits, hurt by the idea of Pitt's alienation." It was to be over two months before they met together again as friends. For many, the reaction of William Windham was typical — a feeling of betrayal and violent anger: "Your friend Mr. Wilberforce," Windham complained to Lady Spencer, "will be very happy any morning to hand your ladyship to the guillotine."

Events in France now worsened and any hopes for peace proved more elusive than ever. However, the spirit in which Wilberforce had acted had done much to prevent a more irreparable breach with Pitt. It also helped change the prime minister's views. One month after they were reconciled, Wilberforce wrote, "All Pitt's supporters believe him disposed to make peace." By the autumn of 1795, all misunderstandings between them were firmly put into the past.

BELOW & RIGHT: Detail of the memorial statue at the Wilberforce House, Hull, the base of which pays tribute to the legacy and achievements of "the friend of humanity."

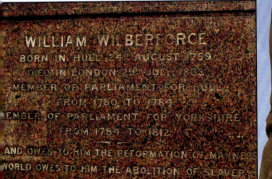

WILLIAM WILBERFORCE
BORN IN HULL 24 AUGUST 1759
DIED IN LONDON 29 JULY 1833
MEMBER OF PARLIAMENT FOR HULL
FROM 1780 TO 1784
MEMBER OF PARLIAMENT FOR YORKSHIRE
FROM 1784 TO 1812

AND OWES TO HIM THE REFORMATION OF MANNERS
WORLD OWES TO HIM THE ABOLITION OF SLAVERY

## Back to Abolition

In early 1796, Wilberforce reintroduced his motion to abolish the slave trade. He spoke "warmly and well," and felt "surprise and joy in carrying my question." A second reading was scheduled for March 3 and passed. However, the third reading of the bill was a disaster! When Wilberforce entered the Commons that evening, a head count indicated he had the votes to end the slave trade. Sadly, this was not the case. The very terseness of Wilberforce's diary entry shows the devastation and hurt he felt: "March 15. Dined before House. Slave Bill thrown out by 74 to 70, ten or twelve of those who had supported me [were] about in the country, or [away] on pleasure. Enough [were] at the Opera to have carried it." Not long afterward he wrote, "I am permanently hurt about the slave trade."

If Wilberforce's sickness in 1788 had brought on torments of the mind and spirit, a first nervous breakdown according to some, this crushing defeat brought on what appears to have been a second one. Shattered in mind and body, he withdrew to the country. Isaac Milner rallied to him, providing medical treatment and comfort. Wilberforce contemplated retirement from politics.

William wrote in this vein to John Newton, who gently but firmly placed everything in perspective. He reminded him that William had a circle of friends who shared his faith and served with him in the Commons; he had also accomplished more good than he knew — less

BELOW: Detail of the courtyard and coach house at Barham Court, a place where Wilberforce enjoyed many rides in the countryside of Kent.

ABOVE: A scence which clearly shows why Barham Court was a place Wilberforce returned to again and again.

61

slaves were allowed to be transported per ship than before; he had for some years demonstrated a consistent, principled character in public life. Then John came to the heart of the matter: "It is true that you live in the midst of difficulties and snares, and you need a double guard of watchfulness and prayer. But since you know both your need of help, and where to look for it, I may say to you as Darius to Daniel: 'Thy God, whom thou servest continually, is able to preserve and deliver you.' Daniel, likewise, was a public man, and in critical circumstances, but he trusted in the Lord, was faithful in his department, and therefore though he had enemies, they could not prevail against him." The old warrior, Newton, went on to remind his younger friend of the many promises of Scripture: "My grace is sufficient for thee," "Without Me you can do nothing," and concluded, "May the Lord bless you, my dear Sir; may He be your sun and your shield, and fill you will all joy and peace in believing."

Newton's letter helped Wilberforce see that he needed to stay the course. Eleven long years lay ahead, but he had come through his crowded hour. He was prepared for the long fight that lay before him. Every year, from 1797–1803, he suffered setbacks. From 1797–1799 his motion was defeated outright. In 1800–1801 it was deferred. No progress was made in 1802, nor in 1803 — when a French invasion was expected. By 1804, however, all indications were that popular support for abolishing the slave trade was steadily growing. The vote was close in 1805. Wilberforce's motion was defeated: 70 for, with 77 against.

### Victory at Last

In January 1806, Pitt died. Wilberforce had lost one of his closest friends. Despite trying differences, their friendship had endured. What no one could have foreseen, not least Wilberforce, was the impact of Pitt's death and the appointment of Lord Grenville as prime minister, for Grenville and Charles Fox, now part of Grenville's cabinet, were steadfastly committed to ending the slave trade. They now moved with all speed.

Wilberforce watched it all unfold. He'd had substantial political differences with Fox and Grenville over the years, but they now worked together as they never had before. When the prime minister spoke against the slave trade in the Abolition Bill debate in 1807, he gave a moving tribute to Wilberforce.

The night of February 23, 1807, was one of the most significant nights in British political history. As Wilberforce's motion was being debated, excitement spread. When one member finished speaking, several others jumped to their feet. Sir Samuel Romilly gave the best speech. He contrasted Wilberforce with Napoleon and the reception each would receive as they returned home. The

BELOW: The Wilberforce Oak, sometimes called Emancipation Oak, on the grounds of Holwood, Pitt's estate near Bromley, Kent.

emperor of France would arrive at the height of earthy ambition — yet also as one who would be tormented by bloodshed and the oppression of war. Wilberforce would return "to the bosom of his happy and delighted family," able to lie down in peace because he had "preserved so many millions of his fellow creatures."

At this, nearly everyone rose to their feet, turned to Wilberforce and cheered. Head in his hands, Wilberforce wept. Beilby Porteus, the Bishop of London, wrote, "They welcomed him with applause such as was scarcely ever before given to any man sitting in his place in either House of Parliament."

ABOVE: John Wesley, from whom Wilberforce received much-needed encouragement in 1791.

Wilberforce later recalled, "I was myself so completely overpowered by my feelings when [Romilly] touched so beautifully on my domestic reception . . . that I was insensible to all that was passing around me."

At 4 a.m. the vote came: 283 for, 16 against. Historian G.M. Trevelyan wrote of what had been achieved:

> Thus was Wilberforce rewarded for his complete honesty of purpose. He had never shrunk from the pursuit of his great humanitarian object even when after the French Revolution it had for a while become extremely unpopular . . . he had always been ready to work with persons of any party, class or religion who would support the cause. He was an enthusiast who was always wise. . . . He could not have done what he did if he had desired [high] office. With his talents and position he would probably have been Pitt's successor as Prime Minister if he had preferred party to mankind. His sacrifice of one kind of fame and power gave him another and a nobler title to remembrance.

Sunday 1787, God Almighty has placed before me two great objects the Suppression of the Slave Trade & the Reformation of manners.

# chapter 5 ■ "I WILL SET ABOUT REFORM"

Some historians have called Wilberforce "the greatest reformer in history." Starting in 1787, he led the fight to end the slave trade, and worked for the remainder of his life to end slavery. He also supported scores of other charitable initiatives. One biographer has written: "Good causes stuck to him like pins to a magnet."

"By God's help," Wilberforce wrote in the autumn of 1787, "I will set vigorously about reform." It was little over a year since the "great change" in his life when he became a Christian, and his understanding of his call to service in political life was sharpening in focus. But what, specifically, should he do? Should he lead the effort to secure the passage of a particular piece of legislation? Or was it perhaps that he ought to spearhead the formation of private, voluntary organizations among the public at large? Throughout the first weeks of the autumn he continued to think and to pray, and he sought the advice of friends. It was Sunday, October 28, 1787, when, after attending church in the morning, Wilberforce met with Newton and made up his mind, writing in his diary: "God has set before me two great objects, the suppression of the slave trade and the reformation of manners."

Wilberforce had embraced evangelical Anglicanism a year earlier, largely through the counsel given him by Newton. It is significant that he, of all people, should have played such a pivotal role in Wilberforce's life — the former slave trader guilty of crimes against humanity, helping to set a protégé on the path of service to humanity — thus ending the slave trade.

BELOW: John Howard, whose important prison reforms influenced Wilberforce.

John Howard
My Hope is in Christ

FACING PAGE: "The greatest mission statement in modern history" — Wilberforce's diary entry setting forth his two great objects: the suppression of the slave trade and the reformation of manners — that is, the work of moral reform.

But what precisely did the "reformation of manners" mean? The key to understanding this second "great object," as Wilberforce had called it, lay in his use of the phase "I will set about reform." He was essentially saying, "Let reform begin in my nation, and let it begin with me." He had himself undergone a great change, and his commitment to Christ showed him what his duties were to God and helped him, increasingly, understand the nature of his duties with regard to his fellow citizens. He put it this way: "It is the true duty of every man to promote the happiness of his fellow-creatures to the utmost of his power."

Wilberforce came to believe that if he did all that he could, in cooperation with others, to help individual Britons come to faith as he had done, the ripple effect of good would spread throughout the kingdom. One by one, more of his fellow citizens would have the hope of heaven in their hearts. They would also be taught by their faith how to show, in practical terms, that they had the welfare of others close to heart. The love of God would best teach them how they could demonstrate their love to fellow human beings.

ABOVE: The Church of All Saints, Wrington. Here the philanthropic legacy of Hannah More and her sisters is cherished. It is also the place where they were laid to rest.

BELOW: The terrace of Barley Wood, the home of Hannah More and her four sisters. Wilberforce visited them often and worked with them in many areas of educational reform.

This led over time to myriad instances of what Wilberforce came to call "concerts of benevolence." In 1808, for example, he wrote to the American president, Thomas Jefferson, suggesting an Anglo-American accord by which both countries would mutually inspect each others ships to ensure that slaves were not being illegally transported to the new world. This "concert of benevolence" was exactly what Wilberforce set in hand in 1787 when he established what became known as the Society for the Reformation of Manners. The story began in 1785 when Wilberforce had become concerned over the signs of cultural decline in Britain that he saw all around him. He wrote to Lord Muncaster:

> It is not the confusion of parties, and their quarrelling and battling in the House of Commons, which makes me despair . . . but it is the universal corruption and profligacy of the times, which, taking its rise amongst the rich and luxurious, has now extended its baneful influence and spread its destructive poison through the whole body of the people.

When it came to the wealthy and those who were among the leadership class, Wilberforce had seen firsthand, for example, the kind of havoc gambling could cause among friends like Charles Fox, who had lost £100,000 (almost 12 million dollars) over the years — a staggering sum. Debauching young women, adultery, and dueling were common. Bribery and corrupt patronage were eating out the vitals of the political system.

The working poor, or "lower orders" as they were then called, were feeling the effects of the early industrial revolution. The flood of people to the great manufacturing centers of Britain had produced terrible social ills. Overcrowding and squalor of the kind that, in the next century, Dickens wrote about so powerfully, were facts of life. Cheap gin was poisoning people by the thousands, who were themselves subjected to dangerous and cruel working conditions in the factories. The church, which some might have expected to serve as a beacon for moral authority, was itself plagued by immorality and apathy, and a mere nominal belief in the Christian creeds was commonplace. It was said that "the spirit of religion slumbered." Many members of the clergy were absent from their churches, often more concerned with hunting and card playing. This led to the neglect of the spiritual and physical needs of their congregations.

Hannah More, the popular playwright who also became a Christian largely through the influence of John Newton, described the church conditions she encountered in rural England about this time. In Axbridge, Somerset, she learned that a preacher named Gould was "drunk about six times a week, has kept a mistress in his house, and very frequently is prevented from preaching by two black eyes got by fighting." High, middle, or lower class — it made no difference — there were crying needs to be met throughout the kingdom. But how to

68

BELOW: Hannah More, the pioneering reformer who was one of Wilberforce's great friends.

ABOVE & BELOW: Cowslip Green as it appears today, the home owned by Hannah More where Wilberforce resolved to sponsor her educational reforms — and Cowslip Green as it was in Wilberforce's day. It is now a private residence.

begin to address them? That was a daunting task.

Wilberforce began to look for historical models that might offer some guide as to how this might be done. He learned of the work that had been accom-

plished during the reign of William and Mary, a century earlier, as a result of a book published by Dr. Josiah Woodward. Its lengthy title states its purpose: *An Account of the of the Rise and Progress of the Religious Societies in the City of London . . . And of the Endeavours for the Reformation of Manners Which Have Been Made therein* (1697). William and Mary had issued a royal proclamation "for the encouragement of Piety and Virtue;

ABOVE: Old Palace Yard, looking NNW, as it was in Wilberforce's time, from a watercolor by Thomas Malton in the British Museum. Also, Old Palace Yard as it looks today. Wilberforce's home would have stood just to the left of the statue of George V.

and for the Preventing of Vice, Profaneness and Immorality." But prior to this proclamation, all across Britain in the 1690s local "Societies for the Reformation of Manners" and "Religious Societies" had been formed. For this reason, the proclamation issued by their majesties had been met with significant success. These societies had devoted their energies to the suppression of public vice, while simultaneously the religious societies had worked to increase the influence of personal faith.

This was exactly how Wilberforce himself felt: "Let reform begin in my nation, and let it begin with me." He was convinced that the government and the reigning monarch ought to affirm the nation's commitment to strengthening its moral consensus, and to issue a proclamation to that effect. At the same time, the citizens of individual towns and cities should assume part of the responsibility for the nation's moral life as well, forming voluntary societies that would encourage people to embrace a faith commitment as he had done, and do what they could on a local level to foster the good of society.

Wilberforce set to work at once, proposing to form a similar association "to resist the spread of open immorality." To his good friend William Hey, a distinguished surgeon in Leeds who was responsible for the founding of the Leeds General Infirmary, he wrote: "Surely it is of the utmost consequence, and worthy of the labours of a whole life."

And so Wilberforce took on a most improbable task — he would act in concert with others to make goodness fashionable. He shared his plan with the Bishop of London, Beilby Porteus, who had already preached a widely influential sermon

William Hey was a close friend and correspondent of Wilberforce and founded the Elland Society to identify poor but promising students and educate them, or as Wilberforce phrased it: "Catching the colts roaming wild on Halifax Moor, and cutting their manes and tails and sending them to college." After studying medicine in London, Hey returned to Leeds to begin his own practice. On his initiative, the building of the Leeds General Infirmary began in 1767. He became senior surgeon there in 1773.

In 1768, with other distinguished physicians in Leeds, Hey founded the Medical Society, and in 1783 he became president of the newly founded Philosophical and Literary Society in Leeds. He practiced medicine for 45 years, and when he died in 1819, Wilberforce lost one of his most valued friends.

on "The Civilization, Improvement and Conversion of the Negro Slaves in the British West-India Islands." Wilberforce also hoped to persuade George III to re-issue the "Proclamation for the encouragement of Piety and Virtue; and for the Preventing of Vice, Profaneness and Immorality" which had marked his accession. Porteus advised Wilberforce about how to implement his plan, and promised to lend his full support to it.

Wilberforce next approached his friends among the

ABOVE: A view from Old Palace Yard which shows its close proximity to Westminster Abbey. Wilberforce's final place of rest is thus quite close to his former residence.

nobility. He secured the approval of Pitt and the Archbishop of Canterbury. By May 29, 1787, Wilberforce was able to report to William Hey:

I trust in a very few days you will hear of a Proclamation being issued for the discouragement of vice, of letters being written by the secretaries of state to the lords-lieutenant, expressing his Majesty's pleasure, that they recommend it to the justices throughout their several counties to be active in the execution of the laws against immoralities, and of a society's being formed in London for the purpose of carrying into effect his Majesty's good and gracious intentions.

Wilberforce next set to work to do all he could to foster the formation of voluntary societies that would further strengthen Britain's moral consensus, serving as a practical complement to the king's proclamation. People at every level would be encouraged to take ownership in this grand scheme: clergymen, working folk, town and city magistrates — all the way up and down the social ladder. And so while Wilberforce started with the leadership class, of which he was a member, he was also instituting a grass-roots campaign. It was a comprehensive plan — an attempt to ask everyone to combine their efforts for the common good.

BELOW: Detail of the plaque which now marks the place where Broomfield stood.

On the site behind this house stood until 1904 Broomwood House (formerly Broomfield) where WILLIAM WILBERFORCE resided during the ✠ CAMPAIGN against ✠ SLAVERY which he ✠ successfully conducted in Parliament ✠✠✠✠✠

BELOW: The architectural plan for Wilberforce's Clapham residence, Broomfield, drawn in 1792.

## The "Minister of Public Charity"

From this began so many of the voluntary societies that were to become in time such a feature of Britain in the years prior to and including Queen Victoria's reign. Organizations

ABOVE: The library at Battersea Rise. Designed by William Pitt, it was the scene of the "Cabinet councils" held by Wilberforce, Thornton, and the others among the Clapham Circle.

like the British and Foreign Bible Society and the Church Missionary Society distributed the Bible and encouraged evangelism. Increasingly, such transformations in the lives of individual Britons helped them to see how they could serve as agents of positive social change. And so, on a practical level, schools for the deaf and blind were established. So too were lending libraries, trade schools, and colleges. Groups arose like the Society for Bettering the Condition and Increasing the Comforts of the Poor — later simply called the Bettering Society. Public health initiatives were undertaken, such as the promotion of smallpox vaccination. Wilberforce worked with the agriculturalist and travel writer Arthur Young to end food shortages. He shared with Jeremy Bentham a plan to aid the poor which so impressed Bentham that the philosopher dedicated an early draft of his "Essay on the Poor Laws" to Wilberforce. Wilberforce also shared his faith with Bentham, who wrote in 1796 to his brother Samuel, "Wilberforce [is] wonderfully cordial and confidential — but is laying plots for converting me — I was hard put to it this morning to parry him." Bentham remained a friend, but did not become a Christian.

A conservative estimate puts the number of charitable causes with which Wilberforce was himself involved at 70. The real number is likely to be far higher, since his involvement with such projects was often anonymous. He served as the vice president of some, a board member or governor of others. Over time, he came to be known as "the minister of public charity." The anterooms of his homes, whether his "parliamentary perch" at Number 4 Old Palace Yard in Westminster, Broomfield in Clapham, or Kensington Gore in later years, became clearing-houses for philanthropy. The headquarters for the "junto," as Wilberforce sometimes called his Clapham Circle friends, was the oval library designed by Pitt at Battersea Rise. The Battersea Rise consultations were once memorably described as "a meeting that never adjourned."

ABOVE: John Quincy Adams, America's sixth president, who had great respect for Wilberforce's reforming labors.

74

The establishment of the National Gallery, the RSPCA, the Bettering Society, groups or legislation that funded the research of scientists such as Sir Humphrey Davy, Michael Faraday, and the physician Edward Jenner — all these and more flowed from "concerts of benevolence" that began with the group of friends at Clapham. The influence of the Society for the Reformation of Manners is seen in the fact that before its dissolution in 1802 it had encouraged many new pieces of legislation into effect.

## A Citizen of the World

Wilberforce also took the golden rule as his mandate and assumed a personal responsibility to love his neighbor as himself — "to do as I would be done by." He visited prisons, at times with Elizabeth Fry, and secured the release of many who had been imprisoned for debt. He visited the sick, including the servants of many friends with whom he stayed over the years. He funded hospitals, saying, "I subscribe to hospitals

ABOVE: View of Clapham Common from the entrance to Holy Trinity Church. Holy Trinity was the spiritual center from which so many philanthropic projects emanated.

and dispensaries with increased good will since I have become a husband and a father." Wilberforce's private secretary, Mr. Ashley, was fond of telling one particular story about Wilberforce's generosity. A naval officer, with a family dependant on him, was in prison for a debt of £80 ($9,600 today). Sir Sidney Smith recommended the officer to Wilberforce, who paid his debt and got him a command. The young officer met an enemy ship, captured her, was promoted, and within a year visited Wilberforce as a newly appointed post captain.

Believing he ought to be a citizen of the world, Wilberforce supported the Friends of Foreigners in Distress, a group whose distinguished members included the Duke of Wellington and John Quincy Adams, America's sixth president. This charity addressed the needs of continental Europeans whose lives had been devastated by war. Adams had huge respect for Wilberforce and was grateful for opportunities of consulting with him "upon subjects so interesting to humanity as those upon which [your] exertions have been so long and so earnestly employed."

In order to be able to give more to those in need, Wilberforce economized in his personal life wherever he could. He sometimes traveled by coach instead of in his own carriage, and in the years before his marriage in 1797, he gave at least one-fourth of his income to charitable groups. He supported members of his extended family, as a letter to the near relation of one cousin reveals:

> Never distress yourself, my dear Mary, on the ground of my being put to expense on account of yourself or your near relatives — you give what is far more valuable than money — time, thought, serious active affectionate persevering attention — and as it has pleased God of His good providence to bless me with affluence, and to give me the power (and I hope the heart) to assist those who are less gifted with the good things of this life; how can I employ them more properly than on near relations . . . on your account I am willing to take the charge of Charles's education for two or three years.

BELOW: A portrait of Wilberforce by Glover.

Wilberforce also gave money to clergymen to support their needy parishioners, and the sons of deceased clergymen, "friendless boys" as he called them, whose school or college education he often paid for. But he gave more than money: he made his house the home of one or two youths, covering the costs of their education. Nor were the poor forgotten; they were invited to join in his family worship on Sunday evening, and he often visited them in their cottages to provide instruction and financial help.

Biographer John Pollock has written that Wilberforce's life "is proof that a man can change his times, though he cannot do so alone." At the close of Wilberforce's life,

ABOVE: Barley Wood, once the home of Hannah More and her sisters, now a private residence. Wilberforce was among its many famous visitors.

crying social needs still existed, but that he and his friends — indeed citizens throughout Britain — had done much to make the country more humane is beyond question.

Thirty-four years after his decision to "set vigorously about reform," Wilberforce reflected:

> It pleased God, to diffuse a spirit. . . . which began to display its love of God and love of man by the formation of societies of a religious and moral nature, which have already contributed in no small degree to bless almost all nations. . . . [Among these are] the diffusion of the Sacred Scriptures, the establishment of societies for spreading throughout the world the blessings of religious light and of moral improvement, the growing attention to the education of our people, with societies and institutions for relieving every species of suffering which vice and misery can ever produce among the human race.

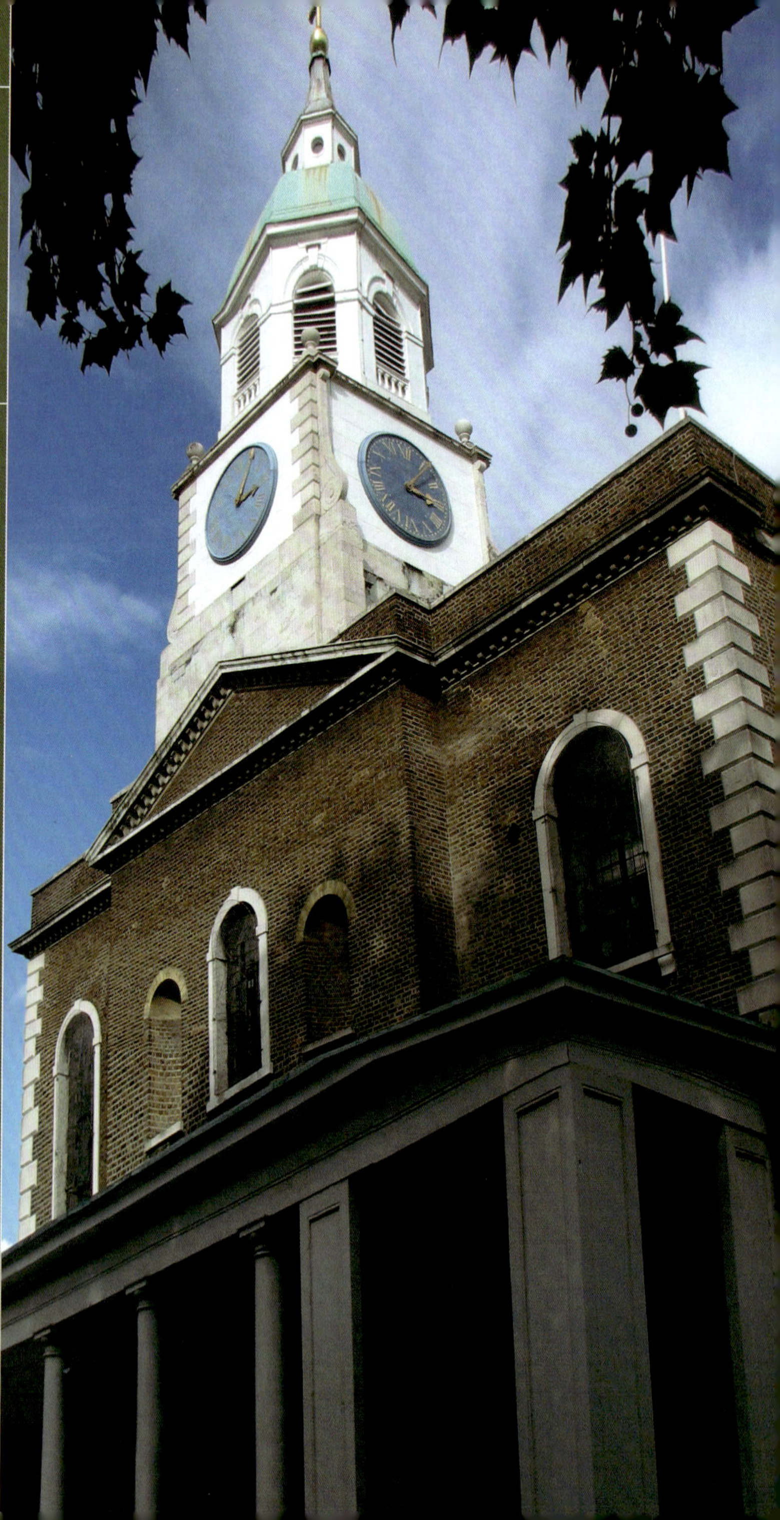

# chapter 6 ■ THE CLAPHAM CIRCLE

The Clapham Circle was a cabinet of philanthropy, an exclusive group of talented men and women in service to Christ and their "fellow creatures." There has never been anything like it before or since.

When Wilberforce moved to Kensington Gore in November 1808, he greatly missed Broomfield, his home in Clapham. It was endeared to him "by much happiness as well as by its own beauty." Parting from his friends there was also close to his heart: "I give up also living near my friends in this circle, yet I trust my connexion with them is so firm that the removal will not weaken it." From this diary entry springs the name of the Clapham Circle, a group that, in the words of John Telford, "moved the world."

All except one of this group were evangelical Anglicans. Their finest moment took place on February 23, 1807. That night, the House of Commons voted to abolish the British slave trade. The Clapham Circle had led the 20-year fight to end it. After the death-knell of the trade had been sounded, Wilberforce and his friends adjourned from the Commons to his "parliamentary perch," but

BELOW: Gore House, Kensington. Wilberforce's home from 1808–1821.

it was actually quite a fine multi-storied structure located at Number 4, Old Palace Yard. It was a triumphant gathering. Wilberforce found it difficult to contain his joy or his boyish

FACING PAGE: Holy Trinity Church, Clapham, the place of worship for Wilberforce and the members of the Clapham Circle.

ABOVE: The grounds and garden of Goer House, the scene of a Horticultural Society exhibition in 1855.

ABOVE: Henry Thornton, the son of John Thornton. Both were members of the Clapham Circle.

ABOVE: John Thorton's villa in Clapham, now a private house.

sense of playfulness. He was nearly 50, but this irrepressible quality had never left him.

"Well, Henry," he said at one point to his cousin and co-worker Henry Thornton, "what shall we abolish next?" Thornton, who was given to a rather serious nature — stepped for a moment out of character. Without missing a beat he said, smiling, "The lottery, I think."

In June 1829, when Wilberforce was elderly and living far from Clapham, he described Clapham as "that honoured and almost hallowed spot." He had begun visiting the then small country hamlet in the late 1780s. His uncle John Thornton (Henry's father) had told him he was welcome at any time to enjoy the hospitality of his red-brick villa, which was on the south side of Clapham Common. Wilberforce came often, enjoying the quiet walks and gardens adjacent to the villa. John Thornton died in 1790, but by this time Wilberforce had also grown close to his son Henry.

William and Henry were cousins, and in the spring of 1792, Henry repeated an earlier suggestion that they could share a large home and its expenses. He had just purchased Battersea Rise, a small estate on the southwest side of Clapham Common. Wilberforce had already experienced the valuable results of annual summer holidays in the homes of two other friends, Thomas Gisborne, a gifted writer, and Thomas Babington, a skilled researcher and MP, and also the uncle of Thomas Babington, Lord Macaulay. At Yoxall Lodge in Staffordshire, Gisborne's residence, and at Rothley Temple in Leicestershire, Babington's home, Wilberforce would study, take long walks, and talk long into the night with his two friends and their families.

Here at Battersea Rise the Clapham Circle was born. There was no great statement of purpose, no grand celebration to get things started. Just two friends, young parliamentarians, seeking friendship in the early days of their political life. At the same time, it is encouraging to note that they had done enough to allow for them both, in the months and years ahead, to grow into the roles for which they had been called. Wilberforce was to write of this many years later: "Of all the manifold blessings which Providence has heaped on me, the greatest of this world . . . consists of kind and intelligent friends, whom He has raised up for my comfort and benefit." Wilberforce always looked back with great fondness to the four-year period when they shared Battersea Rise — "the house . . . [Henry] and I once inhabited as chums . . . when we were solitary bachelors."

Quickly, Thornton realized something more substantial and lasting was arising from what he and Wilberforce had started. He wrote of this in 1793 to Charles Grant (soon to be a Clapham resident):

81

> I am in hopes some good may come out of our Clapham system. Wilberforce is a candle that should not be hid under a bushel. The influence of his conversation is, I think, great and striking. I am surprised to find how much religion everybody seems to have when they get into our house. They seem all to submit, and to acknowledge the advantage of a

religious life, and we are not at all [thought] guilty of carrying things too far.

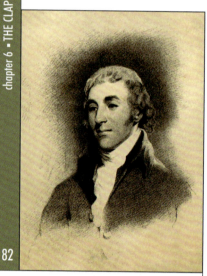

82

ABOVE: Thomas Gisborne, the theologian, philosopher, and poet who was one of Wilberforce's closest friends. The two had been classmates at St. John's College, Cambridge.

Thornton and Wilberforce were, by themselves, something less than what they were together. Over time, they both began to see how they complemented each other. Thornton as the architect — the planner and chairman — and Wilberforce as the minister of hospitality — for his social gifts were such that the Prince of Wales once said that he would go anywhere to hear Wilberforce sing. The French writer Madame de Stael added to the Prince's verdict: "Mr. Wilberforce is the best converser I have met with in this country. I have always heard that he was the most religious, but I now find that he is the wittiest man in England."

One of Wilberforce's younger friends in later life, John Harford, said few "could resist his powers of conversation. . . . it abounded in the anecdotes, reflections, and allusions of a thoughtful mind . . .

## John Thornton (1720–1790)

Though not educated at university, John Thornton had a keen aptitude for business and a vigorous intellect. Family and friends knew him to be a man who was generous and kind, as fond of fun as he was pipe-smoking and talk. A heavy-set man, Thornton's widely known integrity added to the solidity of his nature. He was called an "oak tree of righteousness."

For many years, Thornton was one of Europe's most celebrated philanthropists. He endowed Dartmouth College in America, supported the pastoral ministry of John Newton, and funded the printing of Bibles, which were sent all over the world. Thornton also had a profound influence on both his son Henry and Wilberforce for wise stewardship and benevolence.

ABOVE: Blaise Castle, the home of John Hartford, one of Wilberforce's younger and best friends in later life. Wilberforce loved his "sunny bedchamber" there, and the "oak-fringed knoll in the woods, looking down the glen." BELOW: The castle is now a museum.

whilst it was continually pointed by humour of a most sparkling quality."

Sir James Mackintosh, the most noted conversationalist of the day, and one of Wilberforce's close friends (though they differed widely on some political matters), in 1830, just three years before Wilberforce's death, wrote:

If I were called upon to describe Wilberforce in one word, I should say he was the most amusable man I ever met with in my life. Instead of having to think what subjects will interest him, it is perfectly impossible to hit on one that does not. I never saw anyone who touched life at so many points. . . . When he was in the House of Commons, he seemed to have the freshest

ABOVE: John Hartford, artist, philanthropist, and Fellow of the Royal Society. His *Recollections of William Wilberforce* (1864) showed him to be a Boswell to Wilberforce's Johnson.

mind of any man there. There was all the charm of youth about him. And he is quite as remarkable in this bright evening of his days as when I saw him in his glory many years ago.

Wilberforce's social gifts generated opportunities that would not otherwise have arisen. Because of Wilberforce, Henry Thornton developed a good friendship with Prime Minister William Pitt; a friendship that proved extremely valuable. Thornton, like his father, was a brilliant economist. John Stuart Mill, the political economist, and Nobel Laureate F.A. von Hayek have written compellingly about Thornton's contributions to monetary theory. Thornton had a gift for lucid prose and concise summaries of financial matters. Pitt found in him a trusted advisor and parliamentary colleague. And Pitt, though he perhaps never fully appreciated it, had given to Thornton, Wilberforce, and the other members of the Clapham Circle a gift beyond price — among all his other talents, Pitt designed the magnificent oval library at Battersea Rise where the circle so frequently met. Described as "the solitary monument of the architectural skill of that imperial mind," Pitt's design evoked both beauty and utility.

Pitt's design exceeded the expectations of Henry Thornton and Wilberforce. When the renovations to Battersea Rise began, Thornton also proved something of an architect — and this interest must also have drawn him and Pitt together. Thornton added two wings to the modestly sized three-story villa. Soon a broad hall bisected the house; residents and visitors could view the back

LET VS PRAISE GOD
FOR THE MEMORY AND EXAMPLE OF ALL THE FAITHFVLL
DEPARTED WHO HAVE WORSHIPPED IN THIS CHVRCH AND
ESPECIALLY FOR THE HERE NAMED
SERVANTS OF CHRIST SOMETIME CALLED ·

THE CLAPHAM SECT

WHO IN THE LATTER PART OF THE XVIII.ᵗ AND EARLY PART
OF THE XIX.ᵗ CENTVRIES LABOVRED SO ABVNDANTLY FOR
NATIONAL RIGHTEOVSNESS AND THE CONVERSION OF THE
HEATHEN AND RESTED NOT VNTIL THE CVRSE OF SLAVERY
WAS SWEPT AWAY FROM ALL PARTS OF THE BRITISH DOMINIONS

CHARLES GRANT            HENRY THORNTON
ZACHARY MACAVLAY         JOHN THORNTON
GRANVILLE SHARP          HENRY VENN *curate of Clapham*
JOHN SHORE *lord Teignmouth*  JOHN VENN *rector of Clapham*
JAMES STEPHEN            WILLIAM WILBERFORCE

*We have heard with our ears and our fathers have declared unto us the noble works that Thou didst in their days and in the old time before them*

85

**ABOVE:** The shrapnel-damaged exterior wall memorial for the Clapham Circle at Holy Trinity Church, Clapham — "O God we have heard with our ears and our fathers have declared unto us the noble works that Thou didst in their days and in the old time before them."

garden and lawn from the front door. Tall glass doors opened out onto a grass terrace and behind the glass doors was the library itself with its bookcases all laden with handsome leather-bound volumes. The furniture matched the bookcases and doors, demonstrating the unity of the whole design. Fittingly, there was a bust of Pitt and one of Charles Fox. Taken as a whole, the library was said to have "lent the house half of its charm."

But Henry Thornton was not finished. For his growing circle of friends, he began construction on two other houses — handsome three-storied villas with high Palladian windows and Greek-columned entrances — one on each side of Battersea Rise. Essentially twin houses, they were called Broomfield and Glenelg by those who first lived in them: Pitt's brother-in-law Edward Eliot (also one of Wilberforce's closest friends) and Charles Grant — who had returned to England in 1790 after a distinguished career as a high-level administrator in India. Grant now served with Wilberforce and Thornton as directors of the Sierra Leone Company, chartered in 1791 for the purpose of providing a refuge for freed slaves. Eliot and Grant, like Wilberforce and Thornton, were both evangelicals. The Clapham Circle now numbered four.

The lawns and gardens of Broomfield and Glenelg bordered Battersea Rise. The friends passed easily from one house to another for their meetings "that never adjourned."

By 1793, Eliot and Grant were working with Thornton and Wilberforce to end the slave trade. The "Clapham system," as Thornton called it, was paying deeply important dividends. Grant's experience in India now added another facet to the growing range of philanthropic pursuits of the Clapham Circle. Grant had long supported Christian missions in India. He had seen the linguistic achievements and educational opportunities that missionaries fostered. He was also horrified by human rights abuses he had witnessed: the practices of infanticide and sati (the burning of widows on the funeral pyres of their husbands). Grant's expert testimony, and the immense respect he commanded in the halls of government were to be instrumental in yet another 20-year struggle: that of securing the government's approval of Christian missions in India. This victory was achieved in 1813, aided by Wilberforce, Thornton, and others among the Clapham Circle. The practices of infanticide and sati were not outlawed until 1829, largely through the energies of the Baptist missionary William Carey.

BELOW: William Carey, the missionary pioneer whom Wilberforce so admired. "I cannot," he said, "think of a greater instance of the moral sublime, than that a poor cobbler should have conceived of the conversion of the Hindoos — Milton's composing *Paradise Lost* in his blindness was nothing compared to it."

The Clapham Circle now grew rapidly. William Smith, an MP for the better part of 50 years, had been living in

ABOVE: An engraving from the early 1800s of Clapham Common, with Holy Trinity Church in the background.

Clapham for some time. Unlike the others, Smith was a Unitarian, but that did nothing to preclude the mutual friendship of all concerned, nor their tireless collaboration to end the slave trade. Hour after hour, Smith and Wilberforce examined witnesses for and against the trade. Their collaboration was deeply important to establishing its inhumanity. Smith lived in Clapham until 1812, but his leaving did nothing to diminish his friendship with the circle. He worked with them when community of interests dictated — as with the push to end slavery itself after 1807.

In March 1793, John Venn came to Clapham as rector of Holy Trinity Church, on the north side

BELOW: Sir John Shore (Lord Teignmouth), a member of the Clapham Circle and the first president of the British and Foreign Bible Society.

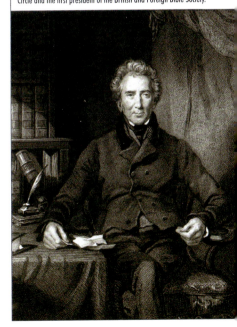

ABOVE: John Venn, rector of Holy Trinity Church. Wilberforce was indebted to him for the gift of his friendship and pastoral counsel.

of Clapham Common. In Venn, the circle gained its parson and Holy Trinity became its spiritual center. Venn, though shy, was a gifted preacher. His sermons attracted such large congregations that the building, capable of seating 1,400 people, sometimes proved too small. However, this was no discouragement. In fact, latecomers in winter sat by the vestry fire listening through the open door. Venn did good service outside of the pulpit as well, helping to found schools and the Church Missionary Society. One summer, Wilberforce and Venn took a holiday together. When Venn died in 1813, Wilberforce knew the bright company had lost one its great lights.

James Stephen joined the circle in 1794, lending his powerful pen and brilliant legal mind to the cause of abolition. It was he who hit upon the legislative strategy that ultimately proved decisive in ending the slave trade. Stephen had seen the horrors of the trade in the West Indies, and could offer vivid, compelling testimony with fire and indignation. Time and again, Wilberforce wrote to him saying how much he valued Stephen's wisdom and forthright counsel. When Wilberforce grew despondent — and he was liable at times to suffer periods of melancholy — Stephen could lift his spirits. Wilberforce wrote to him in 1811: "You are and ever have been kind to me — beyond a brother's kindness — and I think of it often." Wilberforce, for his part, knew how to return the favor. Six years later, in 1817, he wrote this letter:

My dear Stephen,

You appeared to me to look unhappy last night, as if something was giving you pain — either in body

ABOVE: The pulpit in the interior of Holy Trinity Church. The hundreds of sermons preached from it by John Venn were instrumental to the work of the Clapham Circle.

89

or mind. It will be a pleasure to me to hear that this was not so; or if it was, and I can help to remove it, let me try.

  Ever affectionately yours,
  W. Wilberforce

Zachary Macaulay arrived in Clapham in 1799. No matter what the subject or sphere of endeavor, he could seemingly, given time, master it. A short list of his activities reveals his versatility. He was a Fellow of the Royal Society, a successful businessman, active in the British and Foreign Bible Society and the Church Missionary Society. He was the first editor of the *Christian Observer* and wrote many of its articles. He promoted many schools, taking an interest in the educational movements both of Bell and Lancaster, and was one of the principal founders of London University. For five years he was the governor of Sierra Leone, the colony of freed slaves, combining in himself alone the offices of administrator, judge, director of education, and chaplain.

  Macaulay's service to the cause of ending the slave trade and later, slavery itself, was indispensable. His knowledge was so encyclopedic that whenever the circle needed information, Wilberforce would quip, "Let's look it out in Macaulay." He outlived all the other members of the circle, dying in 1838.

Another member of the circle was Sir John Shore (Lord Teignmouth) who lived at Clapham from 1802 to 1808. Once governor-general of India, he and Charles Grant formed a phalanx of compassion for the people of the sub-continent, promoting Christian missions, and seeking to end the practices of sati and infanticide. Lord Teignmouth was also the first president of the British and Foreign Bible Society.

Last, but by no means least, was another honorary member — Hannah More — "the Bishop in petticoats." The schools she and her sisters established in the West Country (funded by Wilberforce and Henry Thornton) educated thousands of children. Her writings — poetry, plays, and a novel, as well as political and theological works — traveled the world and made her a best-selling author. Her vibrant witness touched the lives of the poor as well as the royal family, and her work paved the way for reformers like Elizabeth Fry.

Wilberforce and Thornton commenced funding these schools when Hannah and her sisters lived at Cowslip Green, a cottage near the village of Wrington. Their later home, Barley Wood, was no less notable — described as "the favoured seat of intellectual and religious sunshine." Wilberforce, Thornton, and other friends valued their visits to "the sisterhood," as Wilberforce dubbed them. They called him "the Red-Cross Knight," the character from Spenser's *Fairie Queene* who represented holiness. Together, the

BELOW: Blue plaque for Wilberforce and his cherished circle of friends at Holy Trinity Church, Clapham.

ABOVE: The stone cross that graces the foreground of Holy Trinity Church, Clapham.

sisterhood, their knight, and his round table did much to make Britain more humane.

Together, they established soup kitchens, lending libraries, and schools for the poor, the deaf, and the blind. They sponsored smallpox vaccinations, and worked for shorter working hours and better working conditions in factories. They went into prisons, funded and established hospitals, and purchased the release of those imprisoned for debt. They helped found the Royal Society for the Prevention of Cruelty to Animals and the National Gallery. They wrote books and magazines and distributed the Bible around the world. They sought more humane treatment for Native Americans and the people of India. Above all, without the Clapham Circle the slave trade would not have ended.

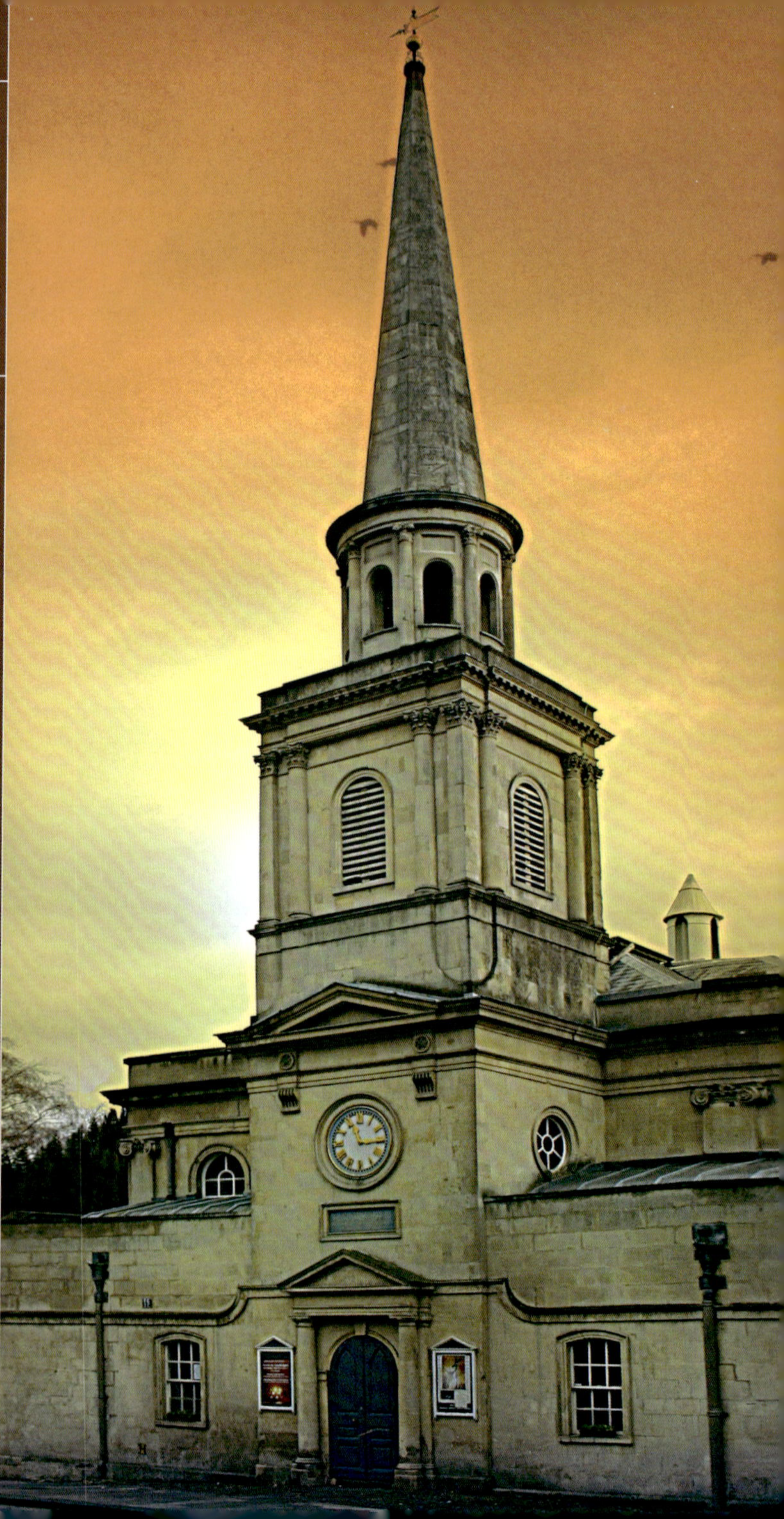

# chapter 7 ■ HOME AND FAMILY

Most of Wilberforce's friends thought him a confirmed bachelor. As he marked his 37th birthday, he thought so, too. Yet it was from the home — among a wife and children he thought he might never have — that one of Wilberforce's lasting contributions to society flowed.

When Wilberforce's sons wrote the biography of their father, they reflected on the home life they had known as children. They compared the man who was known as a bright ornament of society with the way he was among his family: "He was beloved in general society, but if he sparkled there, he shone at home. None but his own family could fully know the warmth of his heart, or the unequalled sweetness of his temper. . . . never . . . did [we] see obscured, in word or action, the full sunshine of his kindliest affections."

Others took note of the relationship Wilberforce had with his wife, Barbara. He was, they all agree, devoted to her. Many Victorian readers of the five-volume *Life of William Wilberforce*, published in 1838, pictured Wilberforce as a model family man. The time he took to be with his wife and children, the ways he invested himself in them, his practice of holding family prayers (a volume of which had been published in 1834), these and other traits made a deep impression on families during Queen Victoria's reign. Yet if we took a snapshot of

RIGHT: Samuel, Wilberforce's third son, about age 25. Later appointed Bishop of Oxford, it was said that Samuel cherished his father's teaching beyond that of any other man.

FACING PAGE: St. Swithin's, the parish church of Walcot. Here Wilberforce and his beloved Barbara were wed in 1797.

his life in, say, 1796, we might never think that Wilberforce would become the husband and family man that he did. At 37, he was to all appearances a confirmed bachelor. However, unlike Pitt, of whom it was said that he was married to his country, Wilberforce seems to have always had a deep longing for a family of his own, though his sense of calling to service in political life prompted within him a struggle as to whether or not he ought to marry. Following his conversion to Christ, friends noted that he far more often thought of others than himself.

ABOVE: Queen Victoria, whose reign was in so many ways influenced by the legacy of Wilberforce.

Seven years before, in 1789, Wilberforce thought he might have found a woman with whom he could build his life, but subsequent events revealed that there was a wide "difference of views and plans of life" between himself and Miss Hammond. Clearly, she did not share his deep commitment to Christianity. Once more he took up his calling to service — perhaps his many good friends would be sufficient. Then, in February 1796, his cousin Henry Thornton married one of Wilberforce's best childhood friends, Marianne Sykes. William saw the love they had for one another and the happy change in their lives, and he began to wish, as he wrote to a friend quoting the poet William Cowper, "not to finish my journey alone." Sometime in the early spring of 1797, Wilberforce began to share his thoughts with his friends. His talks with Thomas Babington, the uncle and namesake of Lord Macaulay, were to prove decisive.

ABOVE: Legh Richmond, author of *The Diaryman's Daughter*, was converted through his reading of Wilberforce's *Practical View of Christianity*.

94

ABOVE: Interior of the Ancient Parish Church of East Farleigh, where Wilberforce heard his son Robert preach at the commencement of his pastoral ministry.

Babington knew of a lovely young woman, Barbara Spooner, who possessed a Christian faith as deep as Wilberforce's own, so he took matters in hand. Babington urged Miss Spooner to write to Wilberforce. She did, and William found her letter charming. On April 13, Babington and Wilberforce met to talk about this very interesting young woman who had so suddenly entered his life. Two days later, Wilberforce met Barbara for the first time. All we know about that meeting is that they fell deeply in love. Politics and charitable projects were set aside for the moment. Those who saw Wilberforce as rather staid and predictable must have suppressed more than a chuckle as they witnessed the whirlwind courtship that he found himself caught up in. His diary entries show that while he was very happy, he wondered if it was all unfolding a little too fast. However, his heart carried the day, and on April 23 he proposed. When he received Barbara's reply later the same day accepting his proposal, he found himself unable to sleep that night.

Wilberforce told his diary: "I believe she is admirably suited to me . . . a real Christian, affectionate, sensible, rational in habits, moderate in desires and habits, capable of bearing

prosperity without intoxication and adversity without repin-
ing." One might be forgiven for thinking that it hardly sounds
like the stuff that dreams are made of. But reading between the
lines, and bearing in mind Wilberforce's subsequent letters to
Barbara, what is clear is that he had found a soul mate — a
friend of the heart — and this is what mattered most to him.

The couple were married on May 30, 1797 — six weeks
after their first meeting! He was 37 and she was 20. A few
months later, Wilberforce wrote a letter to James Stephen
showing how quickly he had settled into happy domesticity. It
was as if he was making up for lost time.

> My plan of life is everywhere the same. The
> morning I spend in some sort of reading and writing,
> taking Mrs. Wilberforce along with me as much as
> I can in my studies and employments. We carry our
> business out of doors, and muse or read whilst tak-
> ing the air and exercise. Dinner and supper are the
> seasons when I enjoy the company of my friends . . .
> I can willingly prolong the dinner conversation till it
> sometimes almost meets the beginning of our supper
> conversation.

## Queen Victoria

In 1798, Wilberforce's *Practical View of Christianity* led a young
curate on the Isle of Wright to faith in Christ. Legh Richmond subsequently
traveled to many villages with the gospel and later wrote stories about his
experiences. The demand for one of these tales, *The Dairyman's Daughter*,
told the story of Elizabeth Wallbridge, a young woman who faced the
prospect of death from consumption (tuberculosis) with great faith and
courage. Translated into five languages, *The Dairyman's Daughter* had
a wide circulation in America. In Richmond's lifetime, two million copies
in English alone were sold, and by 1849, over 4 million copies, in 19
languages.

Around the year 1830, a tourist stopped by the village of Brading on
the Isle of Wright to find the grave of Elizabeth Wallbridge. As he neared
the spot, he saw a lady and a young girl — the latter "reading aloud, in
a full, melodious voice" from *The Dairyman's Daughter*. Not wishing to
disturb them, he decided to visit the site another time; but before leaving
he inquired who the two ladies were, and he learned that the visitors to the
grave were the Duchess of Kent and the Princess (later Queen) Victoria.

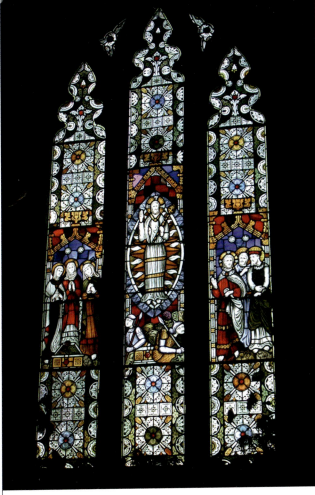

ABOVE: Stained glass window, Church of St. Mary, Brighstone, the church where Samuel Wilberforce commenced his pastoral ministry.

William and Barbara were to share 36 years together. "A more tender, excellent wife," Wilberforce was to say, "no one ever received [as a] gift from the Lord." The children — and Wilberforce had always loved children — came in quick succession. Within ten years, six of them were born. The eldest, William, was born in 1798, Barbara followed in 1799, Elizabeth in 1801, Robert in 1802, Samuel in 1805, and Henry William in 1807. "I could spend hours in watching them," Wilberforce wrote to a friend when speaking of his children. He also loved to play with them. In 1820, when he paid a visit

## Samuel Wilberforce

The faith of the Wilberforce family continued to have important connections to the royal family and to the shape the counsels of the nation in the years after Wilberforce's death. His third son, Samuel (1805–1873), served for a time as chaplain to the House of Lords until he was appointed bishop of Oxford; he later served as lord high almoner to Queen Victoria.

Samuel inherited many of his father's gifts. He was said to have possessed "unfailing tact and wide sympathies, marvelous energy in church organization, a magnetic personality, and great eloquence both on the platform and in the pulpit." His faith found a lasting expression in his classic children's allegories, *Agathos, the Rocky Island,* and *Other Sunday Stories.*

In the House of Lords, Samuel Wilberforce took a prominent part in the discussion of social and church questions. His long-standing interest in charitable trusts, the prevention of cruelty to women and children, the treatment of prisoners, and national education drew forth from him stirring and influential speeches in the House of Lords. In 1854, he founded a theological college in Oxford, now part of Ripon College, Cuddesdon. After 24 years' labor in the diocese of Oxford, he was appointed by Prime Minister William Gladstone to the bishopric of Winchester. He was tragically killed in July 1873, after a fall from his horse.

to the Duchess of Kent, she herself witnessed her guest's enjoyment in children. Wilberforce tells the story. "The Duchess," he recalled, "received me with her fine, animated child on the floor by her with its playthings, of which I soon became one."

When it came to his own children, it was not unusual for Wilberforce to interrupt a letter he was writing because he had been "irresistibly summoned to a contest at marbles." He once seriously injured his leg playing cricket with his son William.

Festive scenes were commonplace in the Wilberforce home. In honor of the coronation of George IV, he provided "ale and cricket to the servants, and all the family." Holiday activities, such as the Twelfth Night party given in 1815, offered a telling picture of the laughter and fun that could be found at Kensington Gore. Wilberforce and his invited guests "all played blind-man's buff for two hours or more." There were also visits "to see some jugglers," or to a toy shop. At other times, Wilberforce would play chess with his children or read to them. Afternoons might find them listening to their father read the Arabian Nights, or in the evenings, Shakespeare. There were visits to the British Museum or home demonstrations of chemical experiments from William Allen — the Quaker chemist, astronomer, and Fellow of the Royal Society.

As his children grew, Wilberforce cultivated his relationship with them by taking long walks or rides with them individually — hiking and garden walks were always favorite activities. He wrote letters to them in which he took great interest in their thoughts and concerns. Over 600 letters to his third son, Samuel, have survived. He also offered encouragement, advice, and expressed a genuine desire to befriend them as they grew into adulthood. Nearly all of them took to his parenting well, though his eldest son, William, was a cause for great concern as he entered his university years. Victorian readers of his biography often modeled their own family life on that of William and Barbara Wilberforce.

Following his retirement from Parliament, Wilberforce spent the spring of 1825 living quietly in his Uxbridge cottage, the Chestnuts, after which he lived at Highwood Hill, in Mill Hill, near Hendon. He had already decided to leave London altogether, and had begun making arrangements to purchase a country home where he hoped to spend the rest of his days. On February 28 he had written to Zachary Macaulay: "It would be a great kindness if you could make out for me anything concerning the plans and intentions of the family of a Mr. Anderson, a sugar broker who died about 10 days ago. I wanted to know whether their country residence at Highwood Hill in Hendon Parish (near Mill Hill) is likely to be sold. I am just come thence."

Highwood Hill, about ten miles north of London and with 140 acres of land, was available, and Wilberforce acted quickly to

BELOW: The letter Wilberforce wrote to Zachary Macaulay, inquiring about the sale of Highwood Hill.

acquire it. It was a lovely residence, having "a good garden pleasantly situated, commanding a very extensive and beautiful prospect; enriched with fine woods." The home itself was a two-story structure, described in 1753 as "a very good brick and sashed house," with wainscoted parlors. Sometime after 1762 it was rebuilt, using stone. The grounds included a garden hothouse, meadow and arable land, a small inn, brewery, farm buildings, brick kiln, a bailiff's house, and dairy.

ABOVE: Blue plaque marking Wilberforce's Highwood Hill estate.

Wilberforce's sons, Robert and Samuel, have left us a word picture of how their father's days at Highwood were regularly spent. He rose soon after seven. After an hour and a half of prayer and devotions, his reader read to him for three quarters of an hour. At half-past nine he led his household in family worship, during which he read a portion of the Scriptures, generally of the New Testament. He then explained the passage, "often with a natural eloquence, always with affectionate earnestness, and an extraordinary knowledge of God's word." A visitor described these times of family worship: "No one could see him as I have done without being charmed. I wish I could send you something of what I have heard in the beautifully simple explanations that he gives every day of a chapter that he reads from the Testament — if you could hear him reading, as he does, the poems in [Keble's] *The Christian Year.* Then he seems so thoroughly pleased to hear any anecdote in praise of any person who is talked about."

This desire of finding some favorable points in every character was noticed by Wilberforce's neighbor, Lady Raffles. She wrote, "I spent a few days at his house, just after Moore's *Life of Lord Byron* was published. I brought it with me from Murray's, and read parts of it to him at night, while he was pacing up and down the room with all the quickness and gaiety of a child. What struck me particularly was his anxiety to find out

ABOVE: A street sign near what was once Wilberforce's Highwood Hill estate.

anything in Lord Byron's favour. 'There now,' he would stop and exclaim, 'surely there is good feeling there!' "

After family prayers, which occupied about half an hour, Wilberforce never failed "to take the air and hear the thrushes sing." He preferred to breakfast late and loved it when friends were gathered round him, and their discussions lasted sometimes until midday. From the breakfast room he went until post time to his study, where he wrote letters. About three o'clock, when the post was gone, he went into the garden alone, humming often to himself some favorite tune. At other times, he walked there with a few friends, or with his reader. During this hour of exercise, he would hold light conversation or draw from his large pockets some favorite volume or other; a Psalter, a Horace, a Shakespeare, or Cowper. He loved flowers and whenever he came in had picked some which he "deposited . . . safely in his room." He stayed out until near dinner, which was never after five, and early in the evening lay down for an hour and a half. He would then sparkle through a long evening to the astonishment of those who expected, at this time of life, to see his mind and spirits flag, even if his strength was not exhausted.

One visitor to Highwood Hill from America described Wilberforce's appearance for us as "altogether peculiar. He was small in stature, extremely rapid in his movements, and crooked almost to deformity. I can hardly say what his countenance would have been in a state of repose, for I think I had no opportunity of seeing it in that state; but in conversation it seemed perfectly radiant with intelligence and benignity."

Even though he had retired from Parliament in February 1825, due to a life-threatening illness in the previous year, Wilberforce continued to do what he could to end slavery throughout Britain's colonies: "We must endeavour to produce throughout the whole country a just sense of our crime in maintaining such a cruel system."

Although his voice had weakened and his body had grown more feeble, on May 15, 1830, William agreed to take the chair at a great meeting of the Anti-Slavery Society. All the old friends of the cause gathered round him. Two thousand people crowded into Freemasons' Hall and hundreds of others had to be turned away at the door.

At the outset of the meeting, Thomas Clarkson rose and made a gracious proposal that Wilberforce should take the chair. William began by looking back with gratitude:

The purpose for which we meet is great — it is urgent; and when I see those by whom I am surrounded — when I again meet my esteemed friend Mr. Clarkson in

BELOW: Robert, Wilberforce's second son, about age 40. In an act of great love, he built a sheltered garden for his father so that he could enjoy the sun and greenery during his final months.

this cause — I cannot but look back to those happy days when we began our labours together; or rather when we worked together — for he began before me — and we made the first step toward that great object, the completion of which is the purpose of our assembling this day.

Wilberforce's involvement in this meeting was an all too brief re-entry into the public arena, but it helped set the stage for the Gen-

ABOVE: The village sign for Mill Hill, a place endeared to Wilberforce as the site of his last home, Highwood Hill.

eral Election of 1830. Four abolitionists were elected to represent Yorkshire, his old constituency. One of them, Henry Brougham, wrote to tell him that the election "turned very much upon slavery; your name was in every mouth, and toasts to your health the most enthusiastically received." This, the last time Wilberforce took any public part in London for the cause, had not been without effect.

For health reasons, the following year he had to decline attending the anniversary of the Anti-Slavery Society. It was a letter he wrote with great regret: "My not obeying the summons issued to assemble in Exeter Hall must be produced by some unavoidable hindrance. The prohibition of my medical adviser is clear and strong. Assure our friends of my best wishes and fervent prayers for the success of our endeavours. Our motto must continue to be, 'Perseverance.' And ultimately, I trust the Almighty will crown our efforts with success." The cause of emancipation was gaining momentum.

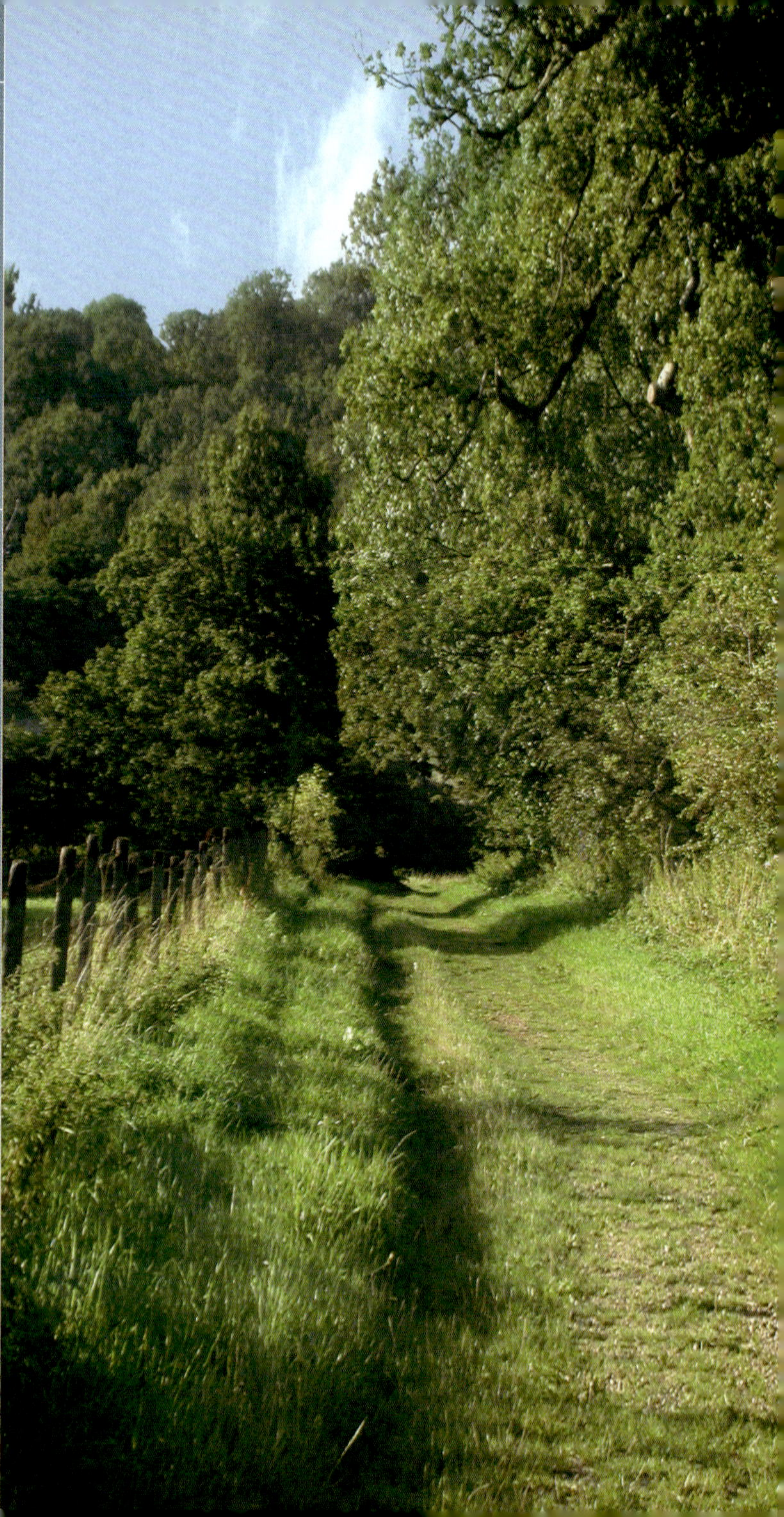

The evening of Wilberforce's days was no less rich or meaningful than his early life. It was a period that attested, as Lord Macaulay wrote, "The abiding eloquence of a Christian life."

How Wilberforce left his beloved Highwood Hill says as much about him as any aspect of his life. The basic facts are these. Wilberforce's eldest son, William, his wife, Mary, and their son — along with their nurse — moved into Highwood Hill in the spring of 1826. Prior to his marriage to Mary Owen, William had been supposedly studying at Trinity College, Cambridge. Instead, his time was spent in excessive spending, constant drunkenness, and deceitful lies to his father. With great sadness, Wilberforce decided to remove him from Cambridge, and after much thought and anxiety, sent him to study law with John Owen, the Secretary of the British and Foreign Bible Society. Not long afterward, William married Owen's daughter Mary. Thus, by 1826, William had married into an evangelical family, brought a grandson into the world, and seemed at last to be settling down.

William was reading for the Bar and was to all appearances applying himself diligently. It was then that the threat of delicate health reared its head, and William

BELOW: Wilberforce in the last year of his life; engraving from a portrait by George Richmond.

105

ABOVE: Bust of Wilberforce by Samuel Joseph. It was sculpted during the last months of Wilberforce's life.

was forced to forgo his studies. Wilberforce now decided that William should farm his fields. There were 140 acres on the estate, and the idea of being able to keep a careful eye on his son must have had some attraction for Wilberforce, a man who devoutly wished to see his son get a good start in life. William was to become a gentleman farmer and enter into partnership with a Major Close to run a large dairy farm. Wilberforce invested significant capital, believing this to be a sound investment financially, and most importantly, in his son's future.

Sadly, by 1829 William's losses were dangerously high and mounting, and by November 1830 he had left England to escape his creditors. With the help of his brother-in-law Richard Spooner, Wilberforce salvaged what could be saved. It was a difficult task. Wilberforce had been giving large sums for about five years to build the chapel that became St. Paul's Church at Mill Hill; he had lowered his tenants' rents substantially, even while continuing to be the largest contributor to charities in and around the city of York; in addition, he had lent Zachary Macaulay £10,000 when his old friend had suffered a loss of fortune. The full extent of William's losses was catastrophic: £50,000, a sum well into the millions in today's currency. How Wilberforce dealt with this blow says a great deal about his courage and the character of his faith. He could have let William take the loss and become an exile on the continent, but he preferred to meet the debt himself.

Wilberforce's friends heard of his fortitude and rallied to him. Many offered to contribute to a recovery fund. Six individual offers were extended to make good the entire debt, including one from Lord Fitzwilliam — formerly one of Wilberforce's greatest political foes, but now a cherished friend. Profoundly moved, Wilberforce said he would only accept contributions to the building fund for St. Paul's. Ever after, he carried a list of these contributors and he delighted in showing it. There was little choice but to sell Highwood Hill. Preparing to leave, he bade farewell to all of his servants, save "a man and a maid and my reader."

He described all that had happened in a letter written on March 16, 1831: "What I shall most miss will be my books and my garden, though I own I do feel a little the not being able to ask my friends to take a dinner or a bed with me under my own roof." Yet there were things for which he felt he could be thankful: His children had all left home by now and "Mrs. Wilberforce and I are supplied with a delightful asylum under the roofs of two of our own children." It was decided that William and

BELOW: Pastures that William Wilberforce Jr. might have farmed.

Barbara would spend half of each year with two of their clergy-man sons — Robert in East Farleigh, and Samuel in Brighstone on the Isle of Wight. "What better could we desire?" Wilberforce reflected. "A kind Providence has enabled me with truth to adopt the declaration of David, that 'goodness and mercy have followed me all my days.' And now, when the cup presented to me has some bitter ingredients, yet surely no draught can be deemed distasteful which comes from such a hand."

However, more tragedy was yet to come. Due perhaps in part to the strain of all that had happened, Wilberforce himself became seriously ill. He did recover, but when he left High-

wood Hill he was still quite sick and weighed little more than five stones (75 pounds). He commented: "I can scarce understand why my life is spared so long, except it be to show that a man can be as happy without a fortune, as with one." But the most difficult trial came soon after he had recovered: his daughter Elizabeth was taken seriously ill and died. During her illness, Wilberforce poured out his feelings on paper: "A holy, calm, humble reliance on her Saviour, enables her to enter the dark valley with Christian hope, leaning as it were on her Redeemer's arm. We are in the hands of our heavenly Father."

Wilberforce's remaining years were those of a pilgrim. The time he spent with his sons became very precious to him. In 1830, Samuel had been appointed Rector of Brighstone on the Isle of Wight, and in 1832 Robert was appointed to the parish of East Farleigh. In the summer, Wilberforce would climb "with delight at Brighstone to the top

108

ABOVE & BELOW: Images depicting St. Paul's Church, Mill Hill — one as it appeared when first completed in 1833, and the other as it appears today.

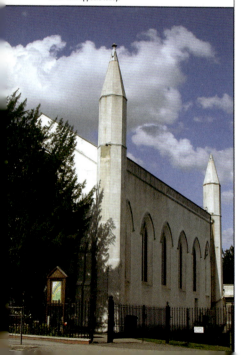

ABOVE: The Parish Church, East Farleigh, and fields beyond.

of the chalk downs, or of an intermediate terrace." As late as 1868, Samuel wrote that this terrace still bore, "in the traditions of the parish," his father's name. At other times, Wilberforce might be found taking long walks on the deserted shore. He became a favorite among the villagers, and local tradition still holds him in memory. One guide reports that "his favorite stroll was up the sunken, fern hung lane and along the crest of Row Down, all among the bracken and bluebells, with larks singing overhead and a wide view over the village to the cliffs and the sea beyond," a path still known as "Wilberforce's Walk"; for some years after, the whole ridge was called "Wilberforce's Down."

Life at the Brighstone rectory held many joys. "This house," Wilberforce wrote, "is enlivened by a delightful infant, which twaddles about most captivatingly, and begins to lisp out 'Papa' and 'Mamma,' with more than Cicero's eloquence. . . .

ABOVE: A thatched cottage in the village of Brighstone on the Isle of Wight.

We should be void of all feeling if the warmest emotions of gratitude were not called forth in us toward the gracious Ordainer of all things, for granting us, in the evening of life, after the tossings of the ocean of this world, such a quiet and comfortable haven. And then that lovely baby!"

The Psalms and St. Paul's Epistles became more and more dear to him. "I find unspeakable pleasure," he told a friend, "in the declarations so often reiterated in the word of God of the unvarying truth of the Supreme Being. To me there is something inexpressibly sublime in the assurance, that throughout the whole immeasurable extent of the . . . empire of God, truth always extends, and like a master-key unlocks and opens all the mysterious wisdom, and goodness, and mercy of the Divine dispensations."

In the rectory at East Farleigh, Wilberforce was said to have found his last real home. He described it as "our delightful quarters," or alternatively, "our much loved quarters." Though his son Robert had only just married Agnes Wrangham and they were expecting their first child, Robert's thoughtfulness could not have been exceeded. Knowing that his father needed exercise in the afternoon, Robert built a garden path for him. There, even in winter, he could enjoy the outdoors. "The gravel walk made expressly for me by dear Robert is extremely valuable," he wrote, "it is so clean and smooth and sheltered." Wilberforce worried that he and Barbara might be proving a burden, but he received "dear Robert's affectionate assurances" otherwise. "Telling me of the pleasure he (and I think he said Agnes also) had in our being with them, quite melted me to tears."

The East Farleigh vicarage was close to Barham Court, the home where Lady and Sir Charles Middleton had lived for so many years. There, almost 50 years before, Wilberforce had been urged to lead the effort to abolish the slave trade. Gratitude to God was, as Samuel Wilberforce wrote, "the chief feature of his later years." One phrase conveyed his gratitude best: "How good a friend God is to me."

## A Portrait of the Old Warrior

Wilberforce still visited Bath for mineral water treatments. His health also permitted him to travel to see his oldest and most valued friends. One visit, in the autumn of 1832, took him back to his old home, Battersea Rise. During his stay, artist George Richmond of the Royal Academy, then just 23, painted his portrait. Wilberforce's portrait was one of his first commissions. It almost didn't happen. Richmond commenced his work when Wilberforce was in conversation, but the quicksilver old politician was seldom still. It was proving impossible to get him to remain in the necessary position. It was then that Charles Forster (grandfather of

BELOW: George Richmond's finished portrait of Wilberforce, 1833.

111

## Three Great Reformers

When Wilberforce died in 1833, one of those who attended his funeral was Anthony Ashley Cooper, the 7th Earl of Shaftesbury, and champion of Britain's industrial poor. Biographer John Pollock wrote, "Thus the two crusades and the lives of two great social reformers touched briefly and symbolically . . . an end and a beginning"

A few weeks earlier, William Gladstone, the future prime minister, met Wilberforce for the first time. And so it was that three great reformers' lives touched briefly. Both Gladstone and Shaftesbury greatly admired Wilberforce. Gladstone wrote about his one and only meeting with Wilberforce. Small kindnesses that showed the young heart of a frail and elderly man stood out.

> In 1833 I had the honor of breakfasting with Mr. Wilberforce a few days before his death, and when I entered the house, immediately after the salutation, he said to me in his silvery tones, "How is your sweet mother?" He had been a guest in my father's house some twelve years before.

Shaftesbury sensed in Wilberforce a kindred spirit. After reading *The Life of William Wilberforce* in 1843, he wrote, "How many things have we felt alike." Others also noted the similarity. In October 1840, the *Times* stated that Shaftesbury was doing for the "slave children" working in Britain's factories and mines what Wilberforce had done for the sons and daughters of Africa.

ABOVE: Contemporary view of the Old Rectory, Brighstone.

novelist E.M. Forster) hit upon the idea of drawing Wilberforce into a fictitious argument. Wilberforce didn't know Forster well, so there was a good chance the ruse might work.

"Pray, Mr Wilberforce," he began as he sat by him, "is it true that the last accounts from the West Indies prove that the slaves are on the whole so much better off than they were thought to be, that you have much altered your views as to slavery?"

"Mr. Forster," Wilberforce replied with genuine emotion, "I am astonished at you. Why would a sensible man like you believe such reports? Why, sir, they flog them with a whip as thick as my arm," grasping it as he spoke.

A most animated debate ensued, and Mr. Forster remained incredulous until Richmond had finished his

ABOVE: The 7th Earl of Shaftesbury — Conservative politician and social reformer.

working sketch. The "happy likeness," as it was called ever afterward, now hangs in the National Portrait Gallery.

On January 1, 1833, Wilberforce wrote a letter to Zachary Macaulay: "I congratulate you, my dear old friend," he wrote, "on having entered on the year which I trust . . . the emancipation of the West Indian slaves [will be] at length accomplished." A few months later, he was encouraged to propose a petition against slavery at a meeting in Maidstone, Kent. He signed it, and it must have been a moving sight to see him making his way forward, perhaps on the arm of his son Robert, to do so. But he did more. Caught up in the spirit of the moment, he decided to make a short speech. His voice might have grown more feeble, but none of his eloquence had left him: "I say, and say honestly and fearlessly, that the same Being who commands us to love mercy, says also, 'Do justice.'" The old warrior for liberty looked round at those assembled: "I trust that we now approach the very end of our career." Suddenly, a ray of sunshine shone through the hall. He seized the moment: "The object is bright before us, the light of heaven beams on it, and is an earnest of success."

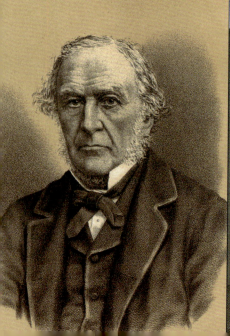

BELOW: Sir William Ewart Gladstone — British Liberal Party statesman and prime minister.

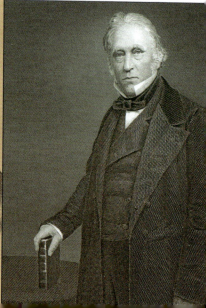

BELOW: Thomas Babington Macaulay, the celebrated writer, historian and politician who was so deeply influenced by Wilberforce.

ABOVE: The Rectory of St. Mary's Church, Brighstone, as it looked in the Late 1800s.

115

On April 20, 1833, Wilberforce left East Farleigh, and after a short visit to the Isle of Wight, arrived at Bath on the 17th of May. It was hoped that the waters might end a bout of influenza, from which he had suffered after leaving Kent. It was not to be. His strength declined. During the two months he spent in Bath, he experienced much pain and weakness.

After two months at Bath, Wilberforce decided to consult Dr. Chambers, an eminent London physician who had treated him with great benefit in 1824. It was a somber journey, for there was little hope that he would recover. Wilberforce intended that he and his family should spend a few days at 44 Cadogan Place, a house lent to him by his cousin, Lucy Smith. He began his journey on July 17, and arrived in London the 19th. On the morning of July 25, Wilberforce's youngest son Henry brought a friend round for breakfast — a young MP named William Ewart Gladstone. The future prime minister wrote of this visit with Wilberforce: "He is cheerful and serene, a beautiful picture of old age in sight of immortality. Heard him pray with his family. Blessing and honor are upon his head."

Parliament was still sitting when Wilberforce arrived in London. Many friends were now able to see him. So too were

ABOVE: The Duke of Wellington — the Iron Duke and hero of Waterloo.

other members of his family, one of whom remembered: "The morning of Friday, July 26th, was pleasant, and I assisted before his breakfast to carry him in a chair to the steps in front of the house, that he might enjoy the air for a few moments. Here he presented a most striking appearance, looking forth with calm delight upon trees and grass. . . . It was nearly his last view of God's works."

That night, the bill for the abolition of slavery was read for the second time in the House of Commons — £20,000,000 (over 2 billion dollars today) would be paid out by the nation to purchase the freedom of those enslaved throughout Britain's colonies. Its passage now assured, the news was rushed to Wilberforce — the last word from Parliament that he ever received. One can only imagine his emotion upon receiving news he had waited for since 1787 — almost 50 years earlier. His first thoughts were of profound gratitude: "Thank God that I should have lived to witness a day in which England is willing to give twenty millions sterling for the Abolition of Slavery."

The following morning he seemed to rally, but toward evening Wilberforce's condition worsened. During the next day, Sunday, July 28, he experienced a succession of fainting fits. That night, when the pain grew great, he spoke to his son Henry: "I am in a very distressed state."

"Yes," Henry replied gently, "but you have your feet on the Rock."

To the last, Wilberforce retained his humility: "I do not venture to speak so positively," he replied, "but I hope I have." He died at three o'clock in the morning on Monday, July 29, 1833.

ABOVE: The old rectory, Brighstone (a private residence).

Almost immediately, the family received a letter from Henry Brougham, the lord chancellor, co-signed by many members of Parliament. It read:

> We the undersigned members of both Houses of Parliament, being anxious upon public grounds to show our respect for the memory of the late William Wilberforce, and being also satisfied that public honours can never be more fitly bestowed than upon such benefactors of mankind, earnestly request that he may be buried in Westminster Abbey; and that we . . . may have permission to attend his funeral.

Thomas Babington, Lord Macaulay, reflected on the death of Wilberforce:

> So Wilberforce is gone! We talk of burying him in Westminster Abbey; and many eminent men, both Whigs and Tories, are desirous to join in paying him this honour. . . . He was cheerful and full of anecdote only last Saturday. He owned that he enjoyed life much, and that he had a great desire to live

longer. Strange in a man who had, I should have said, so little to attach him to this world, and so firm a belief in another; in a man with an impaired fortune, a weak spine, and a worn-out stomach!

The whole of Britain, it seemed, felt his loss. One friend described to Wilberforce's family what he saw as the funeral procession made it way to Westminster Abbey: "You would like to know that as I came toward it down the Strand, every third person I met going about their ordinary business was in mourning."

Another story survived, passed down for years. As the Duke of Wellington walked in the funeral procession, he was recognized by some who watched it pass. They made as though they were going to cheer him. The duke saw it, and before they could applaud, raised his finger to his lips in a silent, but firm admonition. It was, said one who witnessed it, as though the great man were saying: "You are not here to honor me, but him whom I have come to honor."

How does one rightly begin to capture the significance of Wilberforce's life and labors? Historian G.M. Trevelyan described the abolition of the British slave trade as "one of the turning events in the history of the world." In concert with his fellow-laborers, Wilberforce prepared the way for the abolition of slavery throughout Britain's colonies.

But then, there were also scores of charitable works Wilberforce undertook and many acts of humane legislation to which he gave his support.

BELOW: East Farleigh Church spire.

ABOVE: Detail of Wilberforce Memorial, Westminster Abbey.

Publicly and privately, he strove to be a faithful steward, demonstrating what service to something larger than self can mean. Down through the years, many have paid tribute to Wilberforce's life and legacy, perhaps none better than Lord Macaulay, whose words adorn the memorial statue in Westminster Abbey: "In an age fertile in great and good men, he was among the foremost of those who fixed the character of their times — because to high and various talents . . . he added the abiding eloquence of a Christian life."

# A SUMMARY OF THE LIFE OF WILBERFORCE

| | |
|---|---|
| AUGUST 29, 1759 | Born in port city of Hull. |
| OCTOBER 1776 | Enters St. John's College, Cambridge. |
| SEPTEMBER 11, 1780 | Elected MP for Hull. |
| APRIL 7, 1784 | Elected MP for Yorkshire. |
| EASTER 1786 | Completion of his "great change" (embracing Christianity). |
| OCTOBER 28, 1787 | Writes "God Almighty has placed before me two great Objects: — the suppression of the slave trade and the reformation of manners," described as one of the most important mission statements in history. |
| MAY 12, 1789 | Delivers his first great speech against the slave trade. Edmund Burke declares that "it equalled any thing . . . heard in modern times, and was not perhaps to be surpassed in the remains of Grecian eloquence." |
| FEBRUARY 1, 1793 | France declares war on Britain. The conflict lasts 22 years. |
| APRIL 12, 1797 | Publishes *A Practical View of Christianity,* a book greatly praised by the dying Edmund Burke. |
| MARCH 15, 1796 | Devastating, narrow defeat of anti-slave trade bill. |
| MAY 30, 1797 | Marries Barbara Spooner at St. Swithin's Parish Church in Bath. |
| JANUARY 31, 1807 | Publishes *A Letter on the Abolition of the Slave Trade,* which is later translated into French by Madame de Stael at the suggestion of the Duke of Wellington, and distributed by him in France. |
| FEBRUARY 23, 1807 | Passage of bill abolishing the slave trade, called by G.M. Trevelyan "one of the turning events in the history of the world." |

| | |
|---|---|
| MARCH 25, 1807 | Royal assent given to the anti-slave trade bill. |
| SEPTEMBER 1812 | Resigns as MP for Yorkshire, becomes MP for Bramber. Richard Brinsley Sheridan writes to Wilberforce praising his public service. |
| JUNE 22, 1813 | Gives great speech in support of Christian missions in India. Lord Erskine writes that it "Deserves a place in the library of every man of letters, even if he were an atheist." |
| OCTOBER 10, 1814 | Publishes widely influential anti-slave trade letter to Talleyrand, which was circulated in France by the Duke of Wellington. |
| 1822 | Publishes anti-slave trade letter to Emperor Alexander of Russia, which is sent to all the members of the legislatures in France, Belgium, Spain, and Portugal |
| MARCH 1823 | Publishes *An Appeal in Behalf of the Negro Slaves in the West Indies*. Upon reading it, a West Indian planter writes: "It has so affected me, that should it cost me my whole property, I surrender it willingly, that my poor Negros may be brought not only to the liberty of Europeans, but especially to the liberty of Christians." |
| FEBRUARY 22, 1825 | Retires from Parliament. The Poet Laureate Robert Southey writes: "The House of Commons will not look upon your like again." |
| JULY 29, 1833 | Dies in London at 44 Cadogan Place. Thomas Babington Macaulay writes, "He was a very kind friend to me, and I loved him much." |
| AUGUST 5, 1833 | Funeral and interment in Westminster Abbey. He was responsible, it was said, for "saving . . . the soul of the nation." |

# FURTHER READING

Ted Baehr, Susan Wales, and Ken Wales, *The Amazing Grace of Freedom: The Inspiring Faith of William Wilberforce, the Slaves' Champion* (Green Forest, AR: New Leaf Press, 2007).

Kevin Belmonte, *Hero for Humanity: A Biography of William Wilberforce* (Colorado Springs, CO: NavPress, 2002).

Kevin Belmonte, ed., *William Wilberforce, A Practical View of Christianity* (Peabody, MA: Hendrickson Publishers, 1996).

Patrick Cormack, *Wilberforce: The Nation's Conscience* (Basingstoke, Hampshire: Pickering, 1983).

Robin Furneaux, *William Wilberforce* (London: Hamish Hamilton, 1974).

William Hague, *William Pitt the Younger* (London: HarperCollins, 2005).

Garth Lean, *Brave Men Choose* (London: Blandford Press, 1961).

John Pollock, *Wilberforce* (London: John Constable, 1977).

Hugh Thomas, *The Slave Trade* (New York: Simon and Schuster, 1997).

Henry Wheeler, *The Slaves' Champion: The Life, Deeds, and Historical Days of William Wilberforce* (Green Forest, AR: New Leaf Press, 2007).

# THE AMAZING GRACE OF FREEDOM

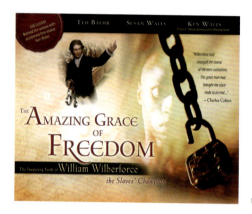

*THE INSPIRING FAITH OF WILLIAM WILBERFORCE, THE SLAVES' CHAMPION*

COMPILED BY

## TED BAEHR, SUSAN WALES, AND KEN WALES

The year 2007 is the landmark 200th anniversary for the Slavery Trade Act, legislation that led to the eventual abolition of slavery in Britain. Spearheaded by the legendary man of faith, William Wilberforce, the legislation marked a victory in the 30-year personal effort to see the brutal captivity and trade of human beings come to an end.

The eventual demise of the British slave trade was a watershed event here in the United States as well. Facing its own conflicts and conflicting legislation on the issue both on the state and federal level in the years 1806 to 1807, the United States lacked a clear, visionary, and moral voice like that which Wilberforce had used so well to win justice for humanity across the sea. As a result, American legislation was passed that was virtually powerless against state laws allowing slavery — setting up a confusing mass of conflicting legal restrictions and loopholes, and inevitably linking the issue of states' rights to that of slavery.

What Wilberforce accomplished peacefully in England would only come to an end in America after the brutal bloody years of the Civil War tore the nation apart. Yet, it would take 100 more years of oppression and prejudice to inspire once again a clear, strong, and moral voice for change before equality would be achieved.

CASEBOUND • 10 x 8 • 144 PAGES • $19.99
ISBN 10: 0-89221-673-5 — ISBN 13: 978-0-89221-673-4

*Available at Christian Bookstores Nationwide*

# THE SLAVES' CHAMPION

*THE LIFE, DEEDS, AND HISTORICAL DAYS OF WILLIAM WILBERFORCE*

## HENRY WHEELER

- Faithfully reproduced from the vintage original
- Gives an intense, spiritual perspective on Wilberforce close to his own time
- Historical facts included with personal information
- A unique study of this influential man of faith and his lifelong fight to end slavery in England

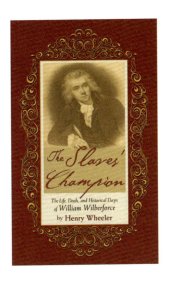

This fascinating book, published in London in 1861, is a revealing biography of British abolitionist William Wilberforce. It includes the reflections of those who knew him and reveals his impact on the final destruction of the brutal slave trade. Correspondence from Wilberforce to his friends and colleagues is highlighted and his Christian character and beliefs are made clear.

Published soon after his death, this book gives a revealing look into the way Wilberforce lived and his impact on British society — an impact that also inspired American abolitionists in their effort to end slavery within the United States. As it was written close to his time, the customs and culture of Wilberforce's era are revealed. *The Slaves' Champion* is a must-read for serious students of Wilberforce and history.

PAPERBACK • 5 X 8 • 240 PAGES • $7.99

ISBN 10: 0-89221-670-0 — ISBN 13: 978-0-89221-670-3

*Available at Christian Bookstores Nationwide*

# WILBERFORCE: AN ACTIVITY BOOK

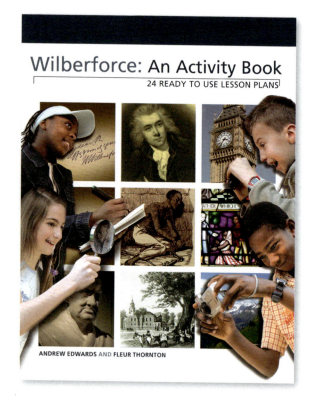

*24 READY TO USE LESSON PLANS*

*BY ANDREW EDWARDS AND FLEUR THORNTON*

PAPER • 8½ x 11 • 32 PAGES • $6.99
ISBN 10: 0-89221-672-7 — ISBN 13: 978-0-89221-672-7

- Fun and educational lessons for elementary students grades 3-5
- A great companion to *A Journey Through the Life of William Wilberforce*, using fun activities to reinforce historical facts.

This educational and fun activity book and guide for elementary age students is a great start for younger children wanting to learn about the fascinating abolitionist William Wilberforce. A great resource for homes and schools alike, this 32-page, fact-filled book features word searches, fact boxes, and so much more. A great way to introduce elementary age students to a man who changed his world and ours. It's "edutainment" of the highest quality.

*Available at Christian Bookstores Nationwide*